Michael Davitt

CLASSICS OF IRISH HISTORY

General Editor: Tom Garvin

Original publication dates of reprinted titles are given in brackets

P. S. O'Hegarty, *The Victory of Sinn Féin* (1924)
Walter McDonald, *Some Ethical Questions of Peace and War* (1919)
Joseph Johnston, *Civil War in Ulster* (1913)
James Mullin, *The Story of a Toiler's Life* (1921)
Robert Brennan, *Ireland Standing Firm* and *Eamon de Valera* (1958)
Mossie Harnett, *Victory and Woe:*
The West Limerick Brigade in the War of Independence
Padraig de Burca and John F. Boyle, *Free State or Republic?*
Pen Pictures of the Historic Treaty Session of Dáil Éireann (1922)
Arthur Clery, *The Idea of a Nation* (1907)
Standish James O'Grady, *To the Leaders of Our Working People*
Michael Davitt, *Jottings in Solitary*
Oliver MacDonagh, *Ireland: The Union and its Aftermath* (1977)
Thomas Fennell, *The Royal Irish Constabulary:*
A History and Personal Memoir
Arthur Griffith, *The Resurrection of Hungary* (1918)
William McComb, *The Repealer Repulsed* (1841)
George Moore, *Parnell and His Island* (1887)
Charlotte Elizabeth Tonna, *Irish Recollections*
(1841/47 as *Personal Recollections*)
Standish James O'Grady, *Sun and Wind*
John Sarsfield Casey, *The Galtee Boy: A Fenian Prison Narrative*
William and Mary Ann Hanbidge,
Memories of West Wicklow: 1813–1939 (1939)
A. P. A. O'Gara, *The Green Republic* (1902)
William Cooke Taylor, *Reminiscences of Daniel O'Connell* (1847)
William Bruce and Henry Joy, *Belfast Politics* (1794)
Annie O'Donnell, *Your Fondest Annie*
Joseph Keating, *My Struggle for Life* (1916)
John Mitchel, *The Last Conquest of Ireland (Perhaps)* (1858/9)
Harold Begbie, *The Lady Next Door* (1914)
Eugene Davis, *Souvenirs of Footprints Over Europe* (1889)
Maria Edgeworth, *An Essay on Irish Bulls* (1802)
D. P. Moran, *The Philosophy of Irish Ireland* (1898–1900)
T. M. Kettle, *The Open Secret of Ireland* (1912)
David W. Miller, *Queen's Rebels* (1978)
Frank Frankfort Moore, *In Belfast by the Sea*
Ernie O'Malley, *Rising Out: Seán Connolly of Longford (1890–1921)*
John Devoy, *Michael Davitt: From the Gaelic American*
Richard Twiss, *A Tour in Ireland in 1775* (1776)

Michael Davitt

From the *Gaelic American*

✦

JOHN DEVOY

edited by

Carla King and W. J. Mc Cormack

UNIVERSITY COLLEGE DUBLIN PRESS
Preas Choláiste Ollscoile Bhaile Átha Cliath

First published in instalments in
the *Gaelic American* in 1906
First book publication, published by
University College Dublin Press, 2008

ISBN 978–1–904558–73–6
ISSN 1393–6883

University College Dublin Press
Newman House, 86 St Stephen's Green
Dublin 2, Ireland
www.ucdpress.ie

Cataloguing in Publication data available
from the British Library

Typeset in Ireland in Ehrhardt by Elaine Burberry
Text design by Lyn Davies, Frome, Somerset, England
Printed in England on acid-free paper by
MPG Books Ltd, Bodmin, Cornwall

CONTENTS

INTRODUCTION

Carla King and W. J. Mc Cormack

On 30 May 1906 Michael Davitt died in the Elpis Nursing Home, Dublin. Ten days later, in New York, John Devoy commenced a series of seventeen articles on Michael Davitt's career in his newspaper, the *Gaelic American*. As biography these are inadequate, focusing as they do only on Davitt's life up to the foundation of the Land League, the period with which Devoy was best acquainted and in which he played an important role. What he does provide is a detailed insight into the world of Fenianism in the United States and Ireland in the 1870s. He also describes the considerations and the efforts behind the New Departure, moves that were to pave the way for that collaboration between land activists, parliamentarians and neo-Fenians in the Land League and its successors, and to culminate in what amounted to a social revolution in Ireland: the ending of landlordism.

Owing both to his longevity and to his decades-long commitment to the cause, John Devoy (1842–1928) was to become the grand old man of Irish Fenianism. Born near Naas, Co. Kildare, he became a Fenian in his teens and then joined the French Foreign Legion to gain military experience. On his return he was directed by James Stephens to enlist in the British Army, where he recruited support for the Irish Republican Brotherhood (IRB) among the soldiers. With the imprisonment of the other Fenian leaders in 1865, he became chief organiser of the IRB until his arrest a year later. Sentenced to fifteen years' penal servitude, he was granted conditional freedom after five years, upon which he emigrated to the United States. Able, dedicated but disputatious, he rapidly emerged as the leading energy behind Clan na Gael, the most important political organisation of radical Irish-Americans. James Stephens is reported to have described the nineteen-year-old Devoy in March 1862 as 'the most stubborn young fellow that I have ever met'.[1] Historians concurred. Thomas N. Brown describes him as 'the ideologue, the Lenin, of Irish-American nationalism',[2] while T. W. Moody saw him as 'the most clear-sighted, pertinacious, and single-minded among the American fenians'.[3]

When Davitt met him in July 1878, Devoy had been settled in New York for seven years, where he worked as foreign editor on the *New York Herald*. Davitt had been released in December 1877, after seven and a half years in prison and travelled to the United States primarily to be reunited with his mother and sisters, whom he had not seen since 1870. On both sides of the Atlantic there was a feeling among some members of the Fenian organisation that the old tactics were in need of modification. As Davitt later put it:

Mere conspiracy had nothing to offer to the mass of the Irish people except the experiences of penal servitude and the records of the abortive rising of 1867. It did not lessen the hold of England upon Ireland in any material way, though the spirit of patriotic sacrifice shown by numbers of young men who cheerfully went to prison in the cause of Irish freedom gave a valuable lesson of fidelity to the ideal of Irish nationhood. Beyond this no more tangible results followed or could proceed from principles tied down to a policy of hopeless impotency; principles which, if only put in action in a wider field of public effort, would exercise a far greater revolutionary influence and power in the contest of nationalism against the forces of English domination in Ireland.[4]

Devoy described the situation more pithily: 'It is time we came out of the rat holes of conspiracy.'[5] It is not true that Davitt conceived the New Departure or the Land League while in prison. However, he was well disposed towards the parliamentarians in recognition of their, eventually successful, efforts to have him released; and he met Parnell, O'Connor Power and several other Home Rule MPs to thank them immediately after leaving prison.[6] More generally, the Amnesty movement had provided a meeting point and opportunity for joint action to parliamentarians and Fenians. In his speeches in Britain in early 1878 Davitt was already calling for harmony and understanding between 'honest home rulers' and 'nationalists' (the term Fenians used in public to describe themselves).[7] But his sojourn in America was to suggest a way forward for nationalism.

Prior to Davitt's arrival in the USA, Devoy's attitude had evolved from the customary Fenian hostility towards parliamentarians, to interest in some co-ordination with them. He was influenced by favourable reports of contacts between Parnell and Clan na Gael envoys. His friend, J. J. O'Kelly, met Parnell in the autumn of 1877.[8] This was followed up by a more formal meeting between Parnell, F. H. O'Donnell and W. H. O'Sullivan on the Parnellite side; O'Kelly and William Carroll from the Clan na Gael leaders in favour of support for the Parnellites; with John O'Leary and John O'Connor representing the Fenian orthodox line, which took place in London in January 1878.[9] Moody suggests that 'Davitt may have been present at this conference and he certainly knew all about it'.[10] Indeed, two months later he attempted, unsuccessfully, to recruit Parnell to the Irish Republican Brotherhood.[11] By the time Davitt arrived in New York in July 1878, there had been a significant shifting of attitudes among Fenians on both sides of the Atlantic, in favour of rapprochement with the more assertive of the Irish parliamentarians.

Shortly after his arrival in America, Davitt was persuaded by the Clan leaders to turn what had been envisaged as primarily a private visit into an extended lecture tour, commencing in September 1878. The holding of public meetings was itself an innovation for American Fenianism and seems to have played an important role in reviving the movement.[12] It was in these months of autumn 1878 that the policy that became known as the 'New Departure' was hammered out in what R. V. Comerford describes as 'a fascinating dialogue-by-speechwriting' between Davitt and Devoy.[13] The outlines of the proposal were encapsulated in the famous telegram sent by Devoy to Parnell detailed below,[14] and of which Davitt learned only later. The despatch of the telegram and the publicity Devoy organised around it were a measure of his political insouciance, Davitt later referring to it as 'a most imprudent proceeding' and 'an illustration of Irish "conspiracy as she was made"'.[15]

But what exactly did the New Departure entail? Moody has pointed out that the three main protagonists left conflicting accounts of it.[16] According to Devoy, in chapters 4 'Davitt's relations with the Fenians' and 5 'Michael Davitt and the Clan na Gael' and 15 'Conditions which Parnell agreed to', below, it was an understanding between Fenians represented by himself and Davitt, on the one side, and parliamentary nationalists represented by Parnell, on the other, and embodied in a secret oral treaty concluded in Dublin on 1 June 1879. According to its terms, Parnell undertook the leadership of the national movement and Davitt and Devoy pledged themselves to secure for him all possible support from the Fenians, in so far as this did not conflict with the aims of Fenianism. In addition, there was agreement that settlement of the land question was to be demanded on the basis of a peasant proprietary to be achieved through compulsory land purchase.

F. S. L. Lyons has suggested that

> to stress the existence of such an alliance was a political, perhaps also a psychological necessity [for Devoy]. Without this to show for his labours he could scarcely have faced his colleagues in the Clan na Gael and without believing that on 1 June Parnell had in effect accepted the 'new departure' Devoy could never have given him the support he consistently did give him during the remainder of his career, even after Parnell appeared to have turned his back on the alliance and all it stood for.[17]

However, both Davitt and Parnell denied that any treaty was ever reached, and it would have been uncharacteristically incautious of Parnell to commit himself in the way described. In Davitt's account the New Departure, as initially conceived, was never implemented. He implies that this was due to opposition from Fenian ranks, spearheaded by Richard Pigott in his paper, *The Irishman*. His chapter on the New Departure in *The Fall of Feudalism* does not mention the meeting of the IRB Supreme Council in Paris in January 1878, where the proposal was formally turned down. But in retrospect he seems to imply that the fact that the new movement was not led by the Fenians was an advantage:

it is perhaps fortunate that the direction of the agitation which has dethroned landlordism and shaken Dublin-Castle rule to its foundations was not taken in hand by those under whose guidance it would have fallen. Neither by temperament nor capacity were they men capable of controlling such a revolutionary spirit as was evoked by the legal and illegal insurrection of the Land League. They were not 'built' that way, to use an expressive American word.[18]

Nevertheless, he recognises that many ex-Fenians were to play important parts in the movement and, in fact, an agreement had been reached in May 1879 that while the IRB would not formally endorse the new policy, individual members would be free to engage in parliamentary politics or agrarian agitation,[19] and many subsequently did so. What remained of his and Devoy's original new departure was their empowerment to take part in the newly emerging land movement. As M. J. Kelly put it:

Above all, the New Departure meant that those Fenians who thought about these things felt able to engage in political activities that did not explicitly repudiate Fenianism's ultimate objectives.[20]

Davitt's account suggests that although the New Departure as initially conceived was not implemented, it was superseded by the collaboration between Parnellite parliamentarians and the Land League that took shape in the course of 1879.

Parnell's version has to be taken with a pinch of salt, as it was given as part of his evidence to the Special Commission on Parnellism and Crime in 1889 where, as Lyons puts it, 'he was fighting for his political life'[21] against those who sought to link the land agitation and parliamentary nationalism with conspiracy to commit violent crime. Not only did he deny that there was any treaty embodying the New Departure, he claimed he had no recollection of meeting with Devoy in 1879, and asserted that the term 'new departure', as he understood it, simply meant 'the combination of the political with the agrarian movement'.[22]

What ultimately drove the need for co-operation was the deepening economic crisis of 1879 and the need to respond to it. Low prices caused by increased foreign competition from lands newly opened by the expansion of railways, coupled with crop failures resulting from adverse weather conditions at home, caused great hardship among Irish farmers. Evictions were rising among tenants unable to pay their rents and a land agitation was commencing in the west, led by men such as James Daly and John James Louden in Mayo and Matthew Harris in Galway. As detailed below, Devoy was in Ireland from April to July 1879, and thus witnessed the birth of the land movement. He was in attendance at the Claremorris meeting on 13 July, the fourth and largest of the series of land meetings from which the Land League emerged. He discusses interviews with Parnell and attempts to persuade him to take leadership of the emergent popular movement. His eventual agreement to do so, and the participation of Fenians and former Fenians in the land agitation, brought forth a united front that was to become a far more formidable force (while it lasted) than the IRB had ever been. It provided Parnell with a mass organisation, lending weight to the Irish parliamentary representatives in voicing the people's grievances. But behind the constitutional movement there was an inherent revolutionary potential. The coalition that constituted Parnell's support in the early 1880s was uniquely powerful, but by definition it was always going to be extremely difficult to control. In this form, it only survived until the Kilmainham Treaty of 1882, following which Parnell dismantled the Land League. Nevertheless, despite the relative passivity of its successor, elements of the earlier combination were to persist.

Comerford has pointed out that there was no inevitability in the class conflict that ensued in the land war. It was, he argues, rather the result of initiatives by elites and individuals endeavouring to use the crisis for their own purposes. He suggests that the landlord–tenant relationship of the mid-1870s, while it differed regionally and locally, and was never an easy one, 'was not self-evidently doomed to disaster'. Moreover, he points out that what eventuated was a form of civil war that had the effect of poisoning both social and economic relationships.[23] Gladstone's government had already shown signs of readiness to embrace reform. Might the conflict have been avoided, and what would have been the outcome if it had? These are questions worth asking but they do not admit of easy answers.

Devoy's memoir, and the tone of the letters from Davitt in 1878, suggest a warm friendship as they formulated their new programme. The two were only four years apart in age, although the older Devoy, who had been at liberty longer and knew America better, had much to teach Davitt. American democracy impressed the younger man and the emphasis on more radical solutions to the land question were characteristic of Irish-American circles, even before the politicisation of land in Ireland.[24] In a heated debate in the press over the months following the proposal of the New Departure, Davitt defended Devoy's character and record against Pigott's insinuations.[25] However, the collaboration of these months was not to last. Davitt's absorption in the Land League distanced him from the Fenians and in May 1880 he was expelled from the organisation. Whereas Devoy welcomed the land movement and defended it as furthering the Fenians' aims,[26] he continued to regard the land question as a means to a future armed rebellion for Irish independence, and never ceased to be a conspirator; Davitt increasingly came to view the overthrow of landlordism as an end in itself. And although he remained loyal to the Fenian policy of abstention from parliament until the 1890s, he came to see peaceful mass politics as far more effective than conspiracy. Fenians were sharply split over the land movement and some never forgave Davitt for what they considered his abandonment of their cause. In April 1880, he was attacked and thrown off the platform at a meeting in the Rotunda, in Dublin. It appears from a letter he sent to Devoy in December 1880 that he was convinced the more hard-line elements were keen to get rid of him.[27] In subsequent years, there were sporadic death threats made against him and efforts to disrupt meetings addressed by him. As late as 1901, there were even threats to assault him if he spoke at the graveside at James Stephens's funeral.[28]

Further divisions between the two followed. When Davitt declared himself publicly in favour of land nationalisation, rather than peasant proprietorship, Devoy was outraged, describing this position as 'a new danger . . . for the Land League'. He claimed its leaders, and presumably he too, viewed Davitt's proposal as 'a complete surrender to England, and an abandonment of the National struggle'.[29] Another dispute occurred over the 'skirmishing fund', a fund established by Jeremiah O'Donovan

Rossa through the pages of the *Irish World*, for the purposes of carrying
out guerrilla warfare against the British Empire. In 1877, the fund was
taken over by a board of trustees representing Clan na Gael and renamed
the National Fund. Devoy, a member of the board, was appealed to by
Davitt early in 1880, not for money as such, but simply for assistance in
organising another lecture tour in the USA, since the money he had
raised in his 1878 tour had now been expended on the Land League.
Devoy's response was to send him $2,000 from the skirmishing fund,
word of which rapidly leaked out in America and subsequently in
Ireland.[30] This connection with a fund aimed at carrying out armed
violence was potentially extremely dangerous for the Land League
leadership striving to maintain the image of the movement as a constitutional one, and indeed the link with the skirmishing fund was to return
to haunt the movement up to and during the Special Commission on
Parnellism and Crime. Davitt, in America a month after the Phoenix
Park murders, moved to limit the damage. In an interview with a
reporter from the New York *World*, he claimed that funding for the Land
League came from the *Irish World* and not from John Devoy, who was
known to be a trustee of the skirmishing fund. Devoy, piqued,
immediately publicly contradicted him, demanding a public retraction.
Shortly afterwards, Davitt repaid the money to Devoy from his own
savings, commenting in his diary:

> Paid Devoy $735 and O'Kelly's promissory note of £50 in liquidation of
> debt of mine to Trustees of National Fund. Thank Heaven I've done
> with *that* infernal transaction. I have never regretted any act of my
> political life so much as that money. *Forced* upon me in order that it could
> be boasted of by those who had thrown sixty thousand dollars away. Am
> almost without a cent today but feel happy in having *that* weight removed
> from me. [William] Redmond present as witness to payment.[31]

From this point, Devoy launched sporadic attacks on Davitt in the
pages of the *Irish Nation*.[32] The final breach occurred over Irish–American
politics, dominated in the 1880s by Alexander Sullivan a Chicago-based
lawyer, who became both president of the Land League and chairman of

the Clan na Gael. Sullivan, described by Professor Moody as 'a sinister lawyer and career-politician, who for a time dominated the Clan [na Gael] in the interests of his republican faction in Chicago politics',[33] had a shady reputation. He and Devoy clashed over his decision to formally dissolve Clan na Gael's fraternal link with the Irish Republican Brotherhood because of the Brotherhood's opposition to the Clan's terrorism campaign. The IRB insisted that the Clan had no right to conduct operations in Ireland and Britain. Devoy had upheld the IRB's right to decide policy in its own sphere and through his branch of the Clan, the Napper Tandy Club, he opposed the severing of ties. Sullivan responded by closing down several protesting branches.

In 1886, when after months of debate the House of Commons rejected the Gladstone's Home Rule Bill, Sullivan and his followers threatened to renew the dynamite campaign in Britain, suspended since 1885. He headed a triumvirate, known as the Triangle, which ran the Clan na Gael, its other members being Michael Boland and Denis Feeley. Davitt, although not one of the official delegates appointed by Parnell, travelled to the American National League's convention in Chicago and succeeded in opposing the return to violence. Prior to the convention he requested a meeting with Devoy, who was also in Chicago, and they lunched together at Davitt's hotel. According to Devoy's account:

> He had very little to say about Ireland, but asked me to give him all the information I had about matters in America. I did so freely and frankly told him all about the split in the Clan na Gael. . . . I also told him of the elaborate scheme to stuff the Convention with Chicago proxies for branches all over the country. . . . I was amazed that Davitt uttered no word of condemnation of this wholly improper and unfair action and I realized that he was irrevocably committed to 'the Triangle' and had completely gone back on his old friends. . . .
>
> We parted as friends, but with a wide gulf between us and we never met again.[34]

Davitt's diary does not mention the meeting, but does record that on his arrival in Chicago he had put Devoy's charges to the leadership of the

League, which they 'unequivocally repudiated'.[35] Nor was he completely in the pocket of the Triangle, as it was mainly with its leader, Alexander Sullivan, that he had to contend in persuading the Clan to desist from a return to the terror campaign.[36]

What were Devoy's intentions in publishing this account of Michael Davitt's career? As he makes clear, he was still bound by the Fenian oath not to divulge detailed information about names or workings of the organisation. Nevertheless, what he relates here is far more extensive than in his other treatments of the subject. One of these, *Land of Eire*, was published under his name in 1882.[37] This is a curious book and Terence Dooley is probably correct in suggesting that only the first 65 pages, comprising Part I, were actually written by Devoy.[38] Here he plays down his own role in the New Departure and omits any discussion of Fenian councils or meetings with Parnell. In fact, apart from the consideration that the remaining 427 pages comprise a traveller's guide to Ireland (implying that Devoy was in the country), there is no reference to his having been in Europe in 1879. A series of articles entitled 'The Story of Clan na Gael', which ran in the *Gaelic American* from 29 November 1924 to 13 June 1925, provides an overview of the history of the organisation but practically ignores the New Departure. Devoy's *Recollections*, published posthumously in 1929, is noteworthy for the little attention it devotes to the New Departure and the emergence of the Land League, moving rapidly from the Fenian movement to the lead up to the 1916 Rising.[39] This series of articles is therefore uniquely valuable in the light it throws on the subject.

Devoy's own explanation for recording the events outlined in his articles is that he was ideally placed to provide such an account:

> I am in a position to prove all this, and, as no living man can be hurt by it and the interests of the Irish cause demand it, I propose to publish the whole story, suppressing such portions only as deal with revolutionary work or affect men still at the mercy of the British Government.[40]

Davitt's death may have set off a series of memories of the heady days of the New Departure, or Devoy may simply have wished to record the events for posterity. The early years of the century saw a depressed period in Fenianism on both sides of the Atlantic. Despite the fact that two warring factions of Clan na Gael were brought together through the efforts of Devoy and Daniel F. Cohalan in 1900, pledged to the use of physical force rather than parliamentary efforts to secure an independent Irish Republic,[41] they represented only a minority fringe within Irish-America. Moreover, as Owen McGee points out, the Fenian organisation on both sides of the Atlantic had long been badly damaged through infiltration by the British Special Branch and its agents, and it was riven by factionalism.[42]

Devoy had launched his newspaper in 1903 to defend the Clan from growing criticisms in the Irish-American press. He had initially planned it as a revival of his paper, the *Irish Nation*, but was prevailed upon by Cohalan, its principal shareholder, to name it the *Gaelic American*, in deference to the growing Irish-Ireland propaganda in Ireland.[43] The articles republished here give the impression that memories and readers' responses encouraged Devoy to continue writing, rather than that the structure of all seventeen was planned in advance. Was publication of these articles on Davitt an attempt to raise morale among the *Gaelic American* readership, mainly members of Clan na Gael, or to bolster Devoy's own credentials among the younger leadership, or again, to reclaim Davitt for the Fenian tradition?

Both Davitt and Devoy in their final years adopted positions they earlier might have thought of as unacceptably moderate. By the end of his life Davitt was no longer a single-minded Irish nationalist and Devoy was willing, by the 1920s, to accept the Treaty. Although temperamentally very different, they were both men of integrity within their different codes.

Obituary

Michael Davitt passes away in Dublin

———————

Michael Davitt, the founder of the Land League, died in Dublin at midnight on Wednesday, 30 May, and was buried in the old family churchyard at Straide, County Mayo, on Saturday last. Mr Davitt had been ill for two months and had been removed to a private hospital where two operations were performed on him.[1] The trouble arose from an ulcerated tooth and blood poisoning set in. Apparently he did not realise the danger until his old friend John Dillon called and noticed that he was suffering from partial lockjaw.[2] The best medical men in Dublin were called in and an operation was decided to, but it was too late. The jawbone became affected and all the doctors could do was to assuage the pain, and when the end came he was free from suffering.

Present at the bedside at the time of death were Mr Davitt's eldest son, Michael,[3] his two daughters,[4] Mr John Dillon and a few intimate friends. Father Hatton had left only a few moments before. Mrs Davitt, who had been in constant attendance on her husband until a few days previously, when she herself was taken ill, was lying prostrate in another room at the time of his death, and the sad news was kept from her for the time being. The greatest sympathy had been displayed by all classes in Ireland during Mr Davitt's illness and all day Thursday the hospital was besieged with anxious callers. Mr Davitt had rallied slightly on Tuesday and the favourable bulletins had raised false hopes of his recovery. During this short rally he was able to speak to those around the bedside, but he soon began to sink again and the doctors, who really never had any hope, prepared his friends for the worst. He died peacefully at midnight on Wednesday.

Mr Davitt left a will which had been prepared for some time and part of the contents of which was made public in Dublin on the day after his death. It leaves all he possessed to his widow (formerly Miss Mary Yore, of Oakland, Cal.)[5] to be disposed of absolutely at her discretion. Mr Davitt died poor, his income being derived solely from his writings, and Land League Cottage, Dalkey, which had been presented to him as a testimonial, is subject to a yearly rent.[6] The will is in part a confession of political faith, one clause of which is a bad setback for those English and Irish newspapers which had with undue haste written homilies on Mr Davitt's 'Complete Version' from extreme Nationalism to some kind of 'Home Rule within the Empire,' and had added sneers at the physical force policy which they claimed Mr Davitt had abandoned for good. The provision read as follows:

'To all my friends I leave kind thoughts, to my enemies the fullest possible forgiveness, and to Ireland my undying prayer for her absolute freedom and independence, which it was my life's ambition to try to obtain for her.'

'Absolute freedom and independence' is the solution of the Irish question which Mr Davitt swore as a Fenian to aid in bringing about, and cannot be interpreted as meaning 'Home Rule within the Empire', the solution sought by the Parliamentary Party. The will also provides that should his death occur in Ireland the burial is to be at Straide, and if in the United States, near his mother's grave at Manayunk, near Philadelphia, and on no account was his body to be brought back to Ireland. If he should die in any other country outside of Great Britain his body was to be buried in the nearest graveyard, but if his demise should occur in Great Britain he must be buried at Straide. The diaries must not be published as such, and in no instance without his wife's permission, 'but on no account must anything harsh or censorious about any person, dead or alive, who ever worked for Ireland be printed or published, or used so as to give pain to friend or relative.'

The English papers commenting on the death make slight allusion to Mr Davitt's political testament and utilise the occasion in a vain attempt to make capital for the Union. As usual in England, some small admissions are made as to England's well meaning mistakes in treating Ireland in the past, but all that is over now and Mr Davitt's 'misguided' course in his youth would have no justification or palliation under the present beneficent regime. The English never miss an occasion like this for lauding themselves, and even the usually level-headed Englishman who sends the weekly cable to the New York *Evening Post* cannot refrain from self-laudation. 'The death of Michael Davitt,' he said last Saturday, 'is the passing of a generation, yet the spirit of the newspaper articles on him shows that the generation had really passed away before him. The references are all moderate and without rancor.' It is only in England that people take credit to themselves for refraining from being rancorous over a man's grave.

The body was taken on Thursday evening from the hospital to the Carmelite church in Clarendon Street and lay there until Saturday morning.[7] It is a singular coincidence that the body of Terence Bellew McManus,[8] one of the Confederate leaders of 1848, which had been brought from San Francisco for interment in Dublin, lay in the same church (instead of at the Mechanics' Institute, as erroneously stated recently in this paper) after Archbishop Cullen[9] had refused to admit it to the Cathedral or to any of the parish churches. The Carmelites, not being under the loyalist Archbishop's jurisdiction, were free to act and retrieved the credit of Ireland. It was John O'Mahony's[10] remains which were waked at the Mechanic's Institute when Cardinal McCabe,[11] following the example of his predecessor, debarred the dead Fenian leader from the Cathedral.

Although Mr Davitt's wish was that the funeral should be private, and every effort was made to comply with his wishes, all Dublin turned out and the whole country was in mourning. The scenes in the streets were very touching as the body was borne on Saturday morning from the Carmelite church, which is on the south side of the Liffey, across the city to the Broadstone Terminus of the Midland Great Western Railway, which is situated at the south-western end of Dublin. The business establishments closed their shutters, the shades were drawn down in the private houses, and the streets were lined by great crowds of people, the men respectfully doffing their hats as the coffin, which was almost hidden by beautiful floral wreaths, was borne by. The funeral procession, which was very large, included many members of the House of Commons, clergymen, and representatives of every religion and political creed. John Redmond,[12] John Dillon and other members of the Irish Party were among the mourners who closely followed the hearse. While the procession stretched out to enormous proportions, another vast crowd awaited the arrival of the body at the station, and on all sides a feeling of the deepest sorrow was apparent among the people.

Numbers of mourners joined the train conveying the body at Mullingar and Athlone. Everywhere hats were respectfully lifted in the fields and on the roadsides as the train passed. An enormous crowd awaited the arrival of the train at Foxford and a procession of vehicles, nearly a mile long, followed by a big gathering of people drawn from miles around, started for Straide, the family burial place of the Davitts, five miles from Foxford.

The old churchyard is near the ruins of one of the Western abbeys.[13] The grave is under an ash tree, within sight of the birthplace of Mr Davitt. A large body of peasantry was waiting at the cemetery and many persons threw wreaths on the coffin when it was lowered into the grave. When all was over a large crowd lingered, their eyes bedimmed with tears, till long after the others had dispersed.

Besides the three children who survive him,[14] Mr Davitt had also another daughter, who died a few years ago. He married Miss May Yore, of Oakland, Cal., in 1887, and his wife shared his popularity and was a devoted believer in all that her husband worked for.

Chapter 1

Michael Davitt's career

The death of Michael Davitt removes from the scene a great national figure, the last of the two greatest men who appeared in the public life of Ireland in this generation. His name and that of Charles Stewart Parnell will be indissolubly linked with the history of the Land League movement, in spite of the bitter antagonism which separated them in the deplorable split which accomplished its ruin and sent its chief to an untimely grave. For, although Davitt was beyond all doubt or question the founder and father of the Land League, and exercised a most potent influence over it to the last moment of its existence, Parnell was just as unquestionably its leader and dominating spirit.

These facts will be apparent to every thinking man who examines critically the history of the movement, not as it has been written by partisans or participators in it, but as it is found in the records from which the impartial future historian must draw his inspiration. And the statement is in no way derogatory to Davitt and detracts nothing from his intellectual power. Mentally he was a bigger man than Parnell; he had an infinitely better knowledge of the Irish people and he had been trained in Fenianism, all of which gave him an advantage over Parnell. But he was by nature an agitator, a preacher of ideas, rather than a politician, and his warm, impetuous temperament and impatience of difference of opinion unfitted him for the difficult role which leaders play in modern popular movements.

Parnell, when he joined the movement, had little knowledge of the Irish people and practically no knowledge of Ireland's history; his only political experience had been in blocking the business of the House of

Commons, and his sole national training was the tradition of an Anglo-Irish landlord family that had been in the Volunteer movement in 1782 and opposed to the Act of Union in 1800.[1] But he had inherited qualities of mind and temper which pre-eminently fitted him for the leadership of a movement with the starting of which he had little to do, and he impressed his personality upon it so strongly that the world speaks of it today as the Parnell movement. And yet Parnell, measured intellectually, was probably inferior to all the great Irish leaders who preceded him, as he unquestionably was to Davitt.

The main facts of Michael Davitt's life are given fairly enough in the obituary sketches printed in the daily papers throughout the country, but the lessons sought to be drawn from it are nearly all absurdly untrue and unfounded. The chief of these is the claim that his life proves that constitutional agitation is more efficacious in obtaining 'reforms' and 'redress of grievances' in Ireland than physical force, and his career as an agitator is used as an argument against Fenianism, in which Davitt received his early training. To sustain this argument the facts are twisted out of their natural shape, the tendency of Davitt's recent speeches and writings is ignored and not a word is said about the very significant reference in his will to the 'absolute freedom and independence of Ireland'.

The truth is that after having changed his early views and given a very long and vigorous trial to constitutional agitation, Davitt was steadily drifting back to the opinions he held as a Fenian when he started the Land League.[2] This sketch will therefore deal chiefly with Davitt as a Fenian, with the facts of the foundation of the Land League and the early relations that prevailed between that organisation and the Fenians, about all of which there is much misrepresentation and still greater ignorance. And the article is signed so that the writer may be held responsible for all that is said.

*

Michael Davitt was born at Straide, Co. Mayo in 1846. His father was a small farmer who was evicted and obliged to go to England to seek a living. The family settled at Haslingden, Lancashire, and at ten years of age Michael was put to work in a cotton factory, where, after a few months he lost his right arm by an accident in the machinery. He was sent back to school for a while and then secured employment with a family that kept a printing office and the local post office.³ This family treated him with great kindness and he ever after spoke of them with affection. Indeed, his personal relations with the English people were always good and for the English working classes he always had a strong sympathy. While in this employment he learned to set type fairly well, attended the local Wesleyan Academy and read every book he could lay his hands upon.⁴ Gaelic was the language of his home, and, although brought up on Lancashire, he spoke Irish pretty well, even when he first began to mix with the people of Connacht. He never acquired, nor tried to acquire an English accent.

When about 17 years of age he joined the Fenian movement, and became very active in the work. Being unable to carry a rifle, he was still determined to take part in the projected insurrection and he went to the attempted raid on Chester Castle in February, 1867, carrying a bag of bullets.⁵

The disastrous split in America⁶ had crippled the movement in Ireland, and the futile attempt to invade Canada in 1866⁷ had dissipated the financial resources which had been the chief hope of the men in Ireland for procuring arms. The decision to fight in Ireland was ill-judged and untimely and was the work of well-meaning men anxious to make good the promises they had made to the rank and file and 'retrieve the credit of the country'. They had not arms enough to put one brigade in the field, and the coolest heads among them were opposed to the rash attempt. And worse still, even those who were resolved to fight were not agreed as to the plan. The result was an abortive attempt to take Chester Castle and a partial rising in Kerry in February, which put the Government thoroughly on its guard and then a more general attempt in Ireland in March after the Government had been fully warned.⁸

There were several thousand rifles in Chester Castle, and a steamer was lying close by on which, if the attack succeeded, they could be conveyed to Ireland with a strong contingent of Fenians from England. But the attack could only succeed by being a complete surprise, and John Joseph Corydon,⁹ a British spy, who had served as a hospital steward in Meagher's Irish Brigade and had been sent to Ireland as an officer, made surprise impossible by informing the Government, which was enabled to take the necessary military precautions.

Captain John McCafferty,[10] who planned the attempt, was the man to carry it out if any man could. He was a Confederate officer, had seen plenty of service in the Civil War with Morgan's guerrillas and had performed many feats of extraordinary skill and daring. One of these was the capture of a quantity of ammunition inside the Federal lines, loading it on a Mississippi steamboat, also captured, and running it safely down the river in face of a sharp fire from the batteries on shore. The men of the organisation in the North of England at that time were mostly young and hardy and were physically fit for any service. Could they have landed in Ireland with arms in their hands they would have made a bright chapter in the history of 'the fighting race', even if they did not succeed in establishing an Irish Republic – and the chance of doing that in the circumstances that then existed was by no means so remote as some of our civilian military critics of today would have us believe.

The attack on Chester was frustrated by Corydon but most of those who had either arrived on the scene or received warning of the failure on their way, were determined they would take part in whatever fight there was going to be, and started by any available steamer for Ireland. They were arrested by the hundred before they could land and thus a considerable contingent of fighting men were [*sic*] prevented from taking part in the rising of 5 March. Others returned to their English homes, and among these was Michael Davitt.

For the first time in Irish history an organised movement for the overthrow of English rule survived defeat in the field. Fenianism promptly reorganised itself and the reorganised movement, while less numerous, was more efficient than that which for ten years had obeyed without question the will of James Stephens.[11] It set to work to repair the damage wrought by the premature attempt at insurrection and to create a system that would endure, no matter what might happen to the leaders or the individual men. And without consultation or concert a similar reorganisation on practically identical lines took place in

America, showing how the race at home and abroad thinks and acts alike in face of similar conditions. In the work of reorganisation at home Michael Davitt took an active part and soon rose to a position of trust and prominence, which, in such cases, is always a post of danger.

Among the men most active in the work of reorganisation was James J. O'Kelly, the present Member of Parliament for North Roscommon.[12] As O'Kelly passed through the ordeal of the Parnell Commission,[13] where his connection with Fenianism was admitted and later published in William O'Brien's paper[14] his recollections of Fenianism (which unfortunately I have not yet read) there is no breach of faith and I feel certain, no violation of his personal wish, in stating here his connection with Davitt. And in order to make my own position clear, I may also briefly allude to my personal connection with O'Kelly. He and I were boys together in Dublin and were sworn into the organisation in the early days of 1861 while attending a Gaelic class which met in the editorial rooms of the *Nation* office,[15] which had been placed at our disposal by Alexander M. Sullivan.[16] When I started to join the Foreign Legion in March, 1861, O'Kelly saw me off at the North Wall, and after I got back he went himself and joined the same regiment, in which he saw hard service in Mexico, where Napoleon the Third was trying to found an empire on French bayonets. He returned when informed by a letter from me, which took six months to reach him, that 1865 had been named as 'the year of action' and resumed his residence in London, where he had practically been the original Fenian in 1862. Among the men O'Kelly brought into the movement in those early days were James Clancy[17] and Joseph J. C. Clarke; the author of 'The Fighting Race', 'Bucky O'Neill' and other poems.[18]

In his work of reorganisation O'Kelly ran across Davitt, was struck with his unusual intelligence and earnestness and at once picked him out for an important and difficult task – that of purchasing and forwarding to Ireland a stock of rifles and revolvers which were to be laid away for future use.

Davitt gave up his employment, undertook this difficult and dangerous work and carried it out successfully for a long time. He employed as his principal agent an Englishman named Wilson who may have suspected, but did not know to what use the rifles and revolvers were intended.[19] In 1870 Davitt and Wilson were arrested, tried, convicted and sentenced to long terms of imprisonment. Davitt made a strong plea for Wilson, assuring the court that the Englishman did not know for whom the rifles were being purchased, and taking the entire responsibility on his own shoulders, but he pleaded in vain and Wilson was sentenced to seven years penal servitude. A year previously a large number of Fenians had been released and in 1871 the remaining 'treason–felony' prisoners were set free, the soldiers of the British army only being still kept in confinement. Davitt remained in prison until 1877, when he was released on 'ticket of leave'.

Immediately on his release Davitt resumed his activity in the Fenian movement and a few months later was elected to the leadership for the North of England. There is no basis whatever for the statements made in recent years that he emerged from prison with changed opinions. By invitation of the Fenians he addressed a series of meetings in Great Britain and Ireland, the proceeds of which were given to the released men, and his speeches at these gatherings, which were well reported in the press, all had the old ring in them. At the private meetings he put himself still more plainly on record, and he would not have been elected a member of the governing body had there been any room for doubt as to his opinions. Davitt came out from his first term of imprisonment a Fenian, just as he had gone in.

His mother was then living in Manayunk and he was anxious to see her before she died. Dr William Carroll, of Philadelphia, made a trip to Ireland and Great Britain in 1877, met Davitt, was very much impressed by him and on his return to America strongly recommended that the Clan na Gael should aid Davitt by getting up a series of lectures that would pay the expenses of his visit and give him a decent sum for himself besides.[20] An official recommendation to the same effect was made by the Fenians at home to their brethren in America.

Having received assurances that he would be welcomed, Davitt started for New York early in 1878.[21] The first man known to him that he saw after landing was O'Kelly, then on the editorial staff of the *Herald*,[22] where I also worked. Within two minutes after he entered the

Herald office O'Kelly called me out and introduced me to Davitt and the following day I started with him for Philadelphia, where at Dr Carroll's house there was a meeting of the governing body of the Clan na Gael in session. A telegram from me had prepared the way, and the reply promptly wired instructed me to bring him on. At that meeting the arrangements were made for a lecture tour under the auspices of the Clan na Gael over most of the United States. That lecture tour was, for those backward days, fairly successful, and besides delivering his lectures in public, Davitt also made speeches at the private meetings of the Clan.[23] He spent the balance of the year making this trip and returned to Ireland on 12 December 1878.

By agreement made with Davitt at a meeting of the governing body of Clan na Gael a few days previously, and at his earnest request, I sailed for Havre on the previous day, to meet him in Paris a few days after our arrival. Davitt, O'Kelly and Dr Carroll saw me on board the *Canada* at 12 o'clock the night before the vessel sailed, that hour being chosen to avoid being recognised and a false name being used on the ticket for the same reason.

What occurred here in America leading up to that trip in Europe, the land propaganda introduced into Davitt's speeches and in still more explicit form in the resolutions passed at the principal meetings, the publication of the 'New Departure' and the events on the other side of the Atlantic which preceded the actual formation of the Land League must form the subject for future articles which many have long been urging me to write and the necessity for which has now come.

I think it proper to say here, however, that I have no desire to imitate Patrick Ford's methods by withholding from him or his paper, the *Irish World*,[24] the credit which belongs to them for helping to make Davitt's lecture tour a success, for the wide publicity given to his meetings and for the no less effective help given in the launching of the new movement in Ireland. I will add, however, that the movement as planned here then, was not to be a mere agrarian one and contemplated as a certain and necessary step to be taken when the situation should have ripened, the withdrawal of the Irish members from the British Parliament.

Chapter 2

Davitt's relations with the Fenians 1

————————

The sketches of Michael Davitt's life which accompany the notices of his death in the leading Irish daily papers are very disappointing. The writing is slap-dash and slipshod, the statements of recent Irish history are inaccurate and the only relieving feature is the sympathy expressed with the dead man and his work. But this very sympathy leads to some of the worst errors of statement.

Davitt is represented as coming out of his first term of imprisonment a full-fledged Land Leaguer, disenchanted with Fenianism and physical force, and a year before the acute distress of 1879 using the distress, which did not then exist, as an argument to win over Irish-America to his new views. He converted us all, it seems, none of us having ever, it must be supposed, read a line of John Mitchel[1] or James Fintan Lalor,[2] and all of us being still full of the impracticable theories of Fenianism. And so the story goes on until Davitt came out here in 1897 and smashed the Arbitration Treaty for us.[3]

This kind of ignorant misstatement and fulsome adulation is, of course, well meant, but it is the reverse of justice to the man. It errs on one side just as ridiculously as the English press does on the other. The *Spectator*,[4] for instance, concludes a short paragraph on his death with this characteristic English snivel:

A good deal of exaggerated language is being used both as regards his abilities and his character, but he was, we believe, a man who, according to his lights, sincerely desired the welfare of Ireland. Unfortunately, he was not able to understand that unless a patriot's methods are as pure as are his ends he will do, not good, but harm, to his cause.

The truth about Davitt's connection and relations with the Fenians at home and the Clan na Gael in America at the time the Land League was founded, or rather from the close of his first imprisonment to his return to penal servitude, is told in his own speeches and letters, as well as in the records of meetings which are still extant. These documents are as authentic as his own diary, or as any other document of the period. A private and most malignant statement already in circulation in New York as to the contents of Davitt's diary makes the publication of some of them necessary for the protection of the National cause. And their publication will put the slanderers and mischief-makers to shame.[5]

The men whom Davitt met at the meeting in Dr Carroll's house in Philadelphia within twenty-four hours of his landing in America, represented the only organised Irish National element in the United States. There were other bodies than the Clan na Gael, some of them large and influential, and their members were full of good will to Ireland, but they did not meet for Irish National purposes and Irish political affairs were not discussed at their meetings. There was a still larger class outside of all distinctively Irish organisations, full of sympathy for their native land, but engaged in no work for Ireland's benefit and having no common ground of action. All of these men were out of Davitt's reach and he was wholly unknown to them.

The only men who knew of him, who worked for the same object as he had at heart, were the members of the Clan na Gael and they alone organised his first course of lectures in America and gave him a platform to stand on from which he could address his countrymen in America. Without their aid he could not have secured an audience at all in the United States and without the proceeds of these lectures – small as the amount was – he could not have devoted his time during the early days of 1879 to the work which he undertook. And, released Fenian as he was, that help would not have been given to him if he had not spoken – in public and in private during his stay in America as a firm believer in the principles and policy for which he had been sent to prison. And the new plank proposed in the Fenian platform was not of his creation, nor of theirs, but was borrowed from the teachings of John Mitchel and James Fintan Lalor in 1848.

Davitt spent a few days with his mother in Manayunk,[6] then returned to New York and delivered his first public address at an excursion of the Irish Volunteers, the military branch of the Clan na Gael, in a grove on the banks of the Hudson.[7] The first of his series of lectures was delivered in Philadelphia on 16 September 1878, and was organised by the Clan na Gael under the direction of William Carroll; an Ulster Presbyterian and intimate friend of John Mitchel. An enthusiastic Philadelphia reporter described Davitt as a 'tall, dark man with a large Websterian head', and this led to his being jocularly called 'Webster' and to his occasionally signing that name to letters to his American friends.

His second lecture was in the Cooper Institute in New York[8] and was preceded by a conference with the Committee – all Clan na Gael men – in Sweeney's Hotel, at which the resolutions were decided on. I drafted these resolutions and proposed them at the Cooper Institute, but John J. Breslin[9] and I had much trouble in convincing Davitt before the committee met that they did not go beyond the bounds of prudence. One of these resolutions demanded National Independence for Ireland, while another declared that 'the land of Ireland belonged to the people of Ireland alone', and that 'the only final solution of the Irish Land Question was the abolition of landlordism and the substitution of a system by which no one would stand between the State and the tiller of the soil – a solution which an Irish Republic could alone effect'.

There was no opposition whatever to these resolutions on the committee and no member of that body considered that there was anything new in them, because they expressed the political faith that all of them already held. The only change from the Fenian policy suggested by the resolutions was in regard to taking part in public agitation, and that was merely going back to the Mitchel and Lalor programme which James Stephens had dropped. Mr Davitt's speech at that meeting in the Cooper Institute certainly outlined in a rather indefinite way a public Nationalist agitation that would include a demand for land reform, but a comparison of it with his later utterances will demonstrate clearly that he had not yet thought out any definite platform or plan of action.

Such conferences as that held with the New York Committee at Sweeney's Hotel took place in every city that Davitt visited. At all these private gatherings he was astonished to find [himself] among men who firmly believed in the physical force policy, and who looked resolutely to Separation as the only solution of the Irish National Question, the most tolerant views with regard to agitations seeking minor objects and the greatest unanimity of opinion as to the necessity of using all such 'peaceful, legal and constitutional' movements for the purpose of developing a sound and healthy public opinion in Ireland. This was largely the effect of their training in American public life. He learned then, what many envoys from Ireland have learned since, that the most extreme Irish Nationalists in America, while ready to adopt the strongest measures against England, were extremely careful to avoid all danger of precipitating premature conflicts at home and took a strictly common-sense view of affairs in Ireland. Among men who believed in secret military preparation – and only secret because necessary – he found also a strong conviction of the absolute necessity of a public National movement in Ireland, in whose ranks the whole people could be enlisted and another necessary part of the work of Irish redemption performed through its instrumentality. In short, he found that men who had gone through a similar experience as himself had arrived at similar conclusions.

A few days after the New York lecture, Davitt delivered another in Brooklyn,[10] at which an incident occurred which shows how far he then was from his later views on the Land Question, and how utterly divergent his opinions were from those of Patrick Ford. Davitt had carefully prepared his New York speech and had read the first draft of it for a few of us, with the result that he rewrote it and made considerable alterations. The references in the first draft to the Land Question were very crude when it came to the proposed remedies. It was a mixture of Sharman Crawford's 'Tenant Right'[11] and Isaac Butt's 'three Fs' – Fixity of Tenure, Fair Rent and Free Sale'[12] – with some provisions of his own to put an end to or curb evictions. By mistake he brought the first rough draft with him to Brooklyn, instead of the finished one, and only discovered his blunder when too late. In speaking he had to refer to the manuscript frequently, holding it in his left hand – the only one that remained to him – and jerking it around nervously. He was naturally very much irritated, and this interfered with his delivery.

In fact, he cut it short and closed abruptly with a discontented look on his face.

It was only about 6 o'clock and the audience wanted more. It was not a large crowd and was mainly composed of old Fenians. Some of them shouted my name and it was taken up vigorously. I had not gone there to speak and was not a practised public speaker, but when Congressman William E. Robinson,[13] who was in the chair, brought me to the front of the platform, I saw the whole Ford family sitting on a front seat. There was a cloud on Patrick Ford's face that presaged a coming storm and he was looking straight at me. I knew that Davitt had brought the wrong manuscript and was therefore at a bad disadvantage but I also felt that if the *Irish World*, which was then read by the majority of Nationalists, should attack him the following week it would be a bad blow. I therefore saw the necessity of retrieving the situation and made a short statement which put our views on land and Nationality more explicitly than even the New York resolutions. Both Davitt's speech and mine – each revised by the speaker – were published in the next issue of the *Irish World*, and reference to them will fully bear out what I have previously said as to how Davitt and the bulk of the American Fenians stood on the Land Question at that time. They are too long to quote here, but I will reprint them at another time.

As we were leaving the hall Patrick Ford met me at the entrance to the platform, shook my hand, and said: 'I congratulate you on that speech. Only for it, I'd feel compelled to denounce Davitt in next week's *Irish World*.' I told this to Davitt on the way back to New York and he resented it. Then and all through his career he was exceedingly sensitive to criticism, and he had in conversation often sarcastically alluded to Mr Ford's lack of acquaintance with Irish affairs (which was very noticeable at that time) and his tendency to take men to task who knew infinitely more than himself. A few weeks later (17 October), writing to me from Cleveland, Davitt added this postscript to his letter: 'That's a damned stupid article in the *World* this week. I mean the leader on Ireland.'[14]

The lecture tour did not in all cases gather large audiences, but except in one case, the net proceeds were all given to Davitt. In some instances the meetings were failures. They were all reported in the *Irish World*, mostly by Davitt himself, and some of them in the *Boston Pilot*,[15] but Davitt's private letters to me gave his personal impressions as he went along and were an unfailing index to the state of his mind and his opinions at the time. One of his worst failures was in New Haven, Conn., where the Clan was then very strong, and where Irish speakers since have mostly fared very well. But Davitt was not daunted at the failure and took comfort out of his meeting with three exceptionally good 'old-timers'. Banteringly, he wrote as follows:

New Haven Ct., Oct. 3 1878

My dear Shane:

Spoke last night with threminjeus effect to, and was listened to with breathless attention by upwards of eight hundred empty seats in Music Hall! Hurrah! Down with the bloody Sasanach!!

Still, although the lecture was a failure, I was delighted with the Sarsfield Club, including such men as Reynolds, Larry O'Brien, Healy and my Connaught co-brick, Pat O'Connor. They were disappointed at the empty house, but your humble servant was prepared for such an event. Spouting is becoming dry and distasteful, and I am not surprised at our people having the good sense to stay at home rather than pay 25 cents to hear England knocked to smithereens and Ireland freed on a public platform.

I spoke to the club privately after the lecture, and its members reflect credit on our movement for their *Sobriety*, intelligence and respectability. I am amply repaid in the pleasure I have in meeting them.

The Providence lecture is abandoned.

Malla more go Dia! A main!!

Yours fraternally,

Mickeen

That kind of reference to the 'private meeting' was continued all through the trip and his own words will show that he took the keenest interest in the revolutionary movement, and only advocated the public agitation at that time as a means of helping the private one. This will be proved conclusively in other articles of this series and by Davitt's own letters – written at the other side of the Atlantic after his return home, as well as in America.

Chapter 3

Davitt and the Fenians

_____

Of all the appreciations of Michael Davitt to be found in the organs of the Parliamentary Party, or written by men who worked with him in the Land and Home Rule movements on the other side of the Atlantic, that of T. P. O'Connor[1] is by long odds the best. Mr O'Connor is seldom held up to admiration in these columns, but his literary skill and knowledge of the world enable him in this case to rise above mere party lines and his eulogy of the dead man can be read with as much interest by those who do not agree with T. P.'s political views as by his most ardent partisans. Every old friend of Davitt, no matter how he may have differed with him, will recognise the truth of this picture of him.

But we all know there are two sides to every man: there are two sides to every story: the side of which the public know, the side of which only those who know the man or the event from the inside really know. In the case of Davitt there was this distinction, that the two sides of the man were to all intents and purposes the same.

The most remarkable and outstanding feature of the man's character is that to the very last he was a transparent child. He was a child in his love of fun, in his keen enjoyment, in his hopefulness, in his simplicity, even in some of his little weaknesses. I dare say he thought himself very shrewd, very secretive, very wary, very Sphinx-like; he was to the end the old conspirator who had to baffle policemen and informers and he therefore gave to himself qualities which he did not possess.

He was, I repeat, a transparent child – fresh from mother earth; like her, naturally joyous and ever ready to recover with the first gleam

of Spring from even a prolonged Winter of trouble, disappointment
and suffering.

And here is another which will be recognised as true by all who knew
him:

> You remembered that Davitt's rages were always of short duration, and
> that he was so true, so honest, and, above all, so loving and lovable, that
> it would be impossible for him to continue long estranged, and if you
> thought of doing so yourself, you laughed yourself out of the absurdity
> of serious anger with this wayward, hot-tempered, lovable child.

Referring to Davitt's depression of spirits in recent years, owing to
his poverty, Mr O'Connor adds this news:

> And then all at once and quite unexpectedly came sunshine. His wife
> had an aunt of considerable means;[2] and when she died it was found that
> she had left to her niece a competency – some three or four thousand
> dollars a year. Davitt was transformed: all his old gayety [*sic*] and hope-
> fulness returned; and he came to London to see his friends and was in
> high spirits.

To understand the difficulties of Davitt's lecture tour it must be
remembered that neither the Clan na Gael nor any other Irish organisation in America had ever undertaken such an enterprise before 1878.
Father Burke[3] and other prominent Irishmen whose fame as speakers
had come before them, had their tours organised by other agencies, but
Davitt was a pioneer in his own line. It was plain sailing in the big cities
of the East, but the smaller towns and the Middle and Western States
where the Irish were not then so numerous were a harder problem.
American Fenianism had reorganised itself, but not for public work, and
the organisation of public meetings was a new thing for most of its
members. The country was full of ex-Fenians, but they were disheart-
ened by the disastrous collapse of the old movement, and the animosities
of the Fenian split had not entirely cooled off. These unattached

Nationalists had to be reached through some other means. Many of them had ceased to read Irish papers but there were many who took the *Irish World*, the *Boston Pilot* or the *Irish-American*.[4] Through the two former mainly the committee sought to reach the Irish-American public.

There was no difficulty whatever in obtaining the support of the *Pilot*, although John Boyle O'Reilly[5] with Patrick A. Collins[6] and Dr Robert Dwyer Joyce,[7] had, in 1876, at the request of Archbishop Williams,[8] dropped away from the Clan, in which O'Reilly and Collins had been officers. My personal intimacy with O'Reilly begun when he was a soldier of the Tenth Hussars and I the Fenian organiser for the British army, and continued to the day of his death, enabled me to win him over to the new public programme at once. He was still a Fenian at heart and was anxious to be doing something, and this programme gave him the opportunity. Before Davitt saw him at all, O'Reilly had given his support to the lecture tour, because Davitt was a released Fenian prisoner, and had talked it up with Collins, Joyce and other friends. Davitt met him in passing through Boston and made a good impression on O'Reilly, although Davitt was somewhat disappointed, so that when they met again on the eve of the Boston lecture, which was held on 8 December 1878, O'Reilly was already a supporter of the new scheme, although he had still much to learn. Davitt, O'Reilly, Dr Joyce and I dined together at Joyce's house in Boylston Street on 7 December, and spent many hours discussing the situation. P. A. Collins was to have been present, but was unable to attend.

So far was the scheme then proposed from being a purely moral force one, looking only to peaceful means for the accomplishment of its ends that a week or so after the conference O'Reilly wrote me a letter which I still have, telling me that he and Joyce had made up their minds to get ready for active service in Ireland whenever the plans had sufficiently ripened. Both of them, he said, had sufficient means to make provision for their families and would be ready to go to Ireland at short notice. In a subsequent interview I had with O'Reilly and Joyce they enlarged on this and they attributed the revival of their fighting enthusiasm to the impression Davitt had made on them. It was a curious fact that Davitt's first impression of O'Reilly was that he did not amount to much,[9] but he soon changed this and fully appreciated O'Reilly's fine qualities. Joyce and O'Reilly were disappointed when I explained to them that the fighting stage was still a long way off.

The *Irish World* reached a different set of people from those who read the *Pilot*. The latter included many priests and prosperous business men, while the *Irish World* circulated chiefly among the working people of Irish race. It could not be said to be a Nationalist paper or committed to any definite solution of the Irish Question, but it was fiercely anti-English, and assailed the landlords in vigorous, but not very clear language. The 'Great Blasphemy' constantly referred to in its editorials was supposed to mean private ownership in land, but one might wade through many columns of invective without ascertaining how it was proposed to settle the question. 'Transatlantic', a man of mystery said by some veterans of 1848 to have had a good reason for concealing his identity, gave instructions every week which included everything needed for Irish regeneration, from the making of a bomb to the construction of an Irish constitution.[10] His articles were the chief attraction in the paper, and thousands of sturdy men of the less intelligent kind believed implicitly in him as the apostle of a new and regenerated Ireland.

Patrick Ford had kept aloof from Fenianism and looked on it with contempt. He knew little of actual conditions in Ireland, but there was no mistaking the sincerity of his belief that English government in Ireland was all wrong and ought to be overturned by some means or other. I introduced Davitt to him and he received him cordially and was much interested in him. He listened patiently to the exposition of the new scheme, but did not at first like some of its features, especially the parliamentary one and the interference in municipal elections. On one occasion he asked me was I sure that any city in Ireland had the right to elect its own Council, and on my assurance that they had, he asked me had I ever seen such an election. I assured him that I had, but he evidently thought I must be mistaken.[11] However, the anti-landlord part of the programme he was in full sympathy with, though I think he did not regard peasant proprietary as a final solution. But, no matter what reservations he may have had, he agreed to open his columns to the new propaganda, and he loyally kept his word during the whole of Davitt's tour, and published good reports of all his meetings.

This support, coupled with that of the Boston *Pilot*, was of great use in placing the movement before the public. It is proper to say here also that through the news columns of the New York *Herald*, then the foremost American journal, we were able occasionally to reach a much larger portion of the general public than could be done through any Irish paper. The *Herald*'s staff was then largely Irish. Thomas B. Connery[12] was Managing Editor, Joseph I. C. Clarke was sometimes Night Editor and at others an editorial writer. Jerome J. Collins,[13] the founder of Clan na Gael, had charge of its meteorological department and wrote editorials besides. O'Kelly was the dramatic critic. I had charge of the foreign desk and fully three-fourths of the reporters were Irish either by birth or parentage. T. P. O'Connor about that time worked in the London office, and I often edited his copy, but he never touched Irish subjects. While perfectly loyal to the paper we were able by supplying it with exclusive news to make it the medium of an Irish propaganda, and at that time we had friends on all the daily papers – Walter O'Dwyer was on the *Tribune*,[14] John C. Hennessy on the *Times*,[15] John Gallagher on the *World*, while Amos J. Cummings, whose mother was Irish, opened the *Sun's* columns to us, Charles A. Dane himself being very decidedly friendly.[16] All these Irish journalists whom I have named were men whose word would be taken by the city editors of the papers on which they worked on a matter of Irish news, and, as the news in this case was genuine: the city editors were glad to get it. I kept in consistent touch with my newspaper friends and in most cases wrote the reports myself for all of them.

The daily papers in those days often attacked Irishmen engaged in American politics – and they often deserved to be attacked – but Irish Nationalists were nearly always treated with respect. The change for the worse which has taken place since then is very largely the fault of Irishmen themselves. The assaults on prominent Nationalists, the 'exposures' and the mudslinging are all the work of Irish blackguards, and the new journalism regards that kind of stuff as the only genuine Irish 'news'.

It is not necessary to go over the history of Davitt's whole lecture tour, but his impressions of the men he met and of the conditions he found, as well as of the state of his own mind at the time, will be best told by some of his letters. Passing through New York, between lectures, he left this hurried note, written in pencil and without date, at Sweeney's Hotel for me, as he was starting off again:

Dear John – I slept till six this morning and have not much time to spare. I am sorry I could not keep awake until you came back from the office. I have not the conscience to disturb you this morning, even for the gratification of a shake hands, before I go, as you are simply worked out of all reasonable rest by one thing or another. Try and get M—[17] out of this hotel if possible. Some private lodgings would be more suitable. Don't forget the thing you spoke of last night, *in re* the Brooklyn men's desire to have an explanation of why the money is still kept in ——'s hands. I ventured to hint at the necessity of a circular in a hurried note to the Doctor, and a word from yourself would set him going at once. Thanks for the addresses and note.

Yours fraternally,

Michael

I leave you the manuscript of the lecture to do as you please with it.

Davitt's active interest in the revolutionary organisation at this period and his intense desire to see it placed in a sound and healthy condition are shown by the following letter from Cleveland:

Striebinger House,
Cleveland, O., 17 October 1878

My dear Shawn – I called at the Albany, Little Falls, Rochester and Buffalo en route for this city. I am to see the clubs in Albany on my return – have had a promise that something will be started in Little Falls ere long. Saw the club in Rochester and found out two of a defunct club in Buffalo last night. I am to return through that city and all the old club is to be assembled on the occasion. I like Mahon.[18] He is a man of sound good judgment. The Rochester men are a credit to our firm. A poor fellow who saw me in York (England) ten years ago met me at the station at five this morning.

Walsh will be here in an hour. The weather is in anti-lecture state, and empty benches will be in the majority tonight. I am heartily sick of *public* spouting and wish I had never consented to anything but *private* 'oratory'. However, another month may see the end of it.

Yours fraternally,

Michael

That's a damned stupid article in the *World* this week. I mean the leader on 'Ireland'.

Chapter 4

Davitt's relations with the Fenians 11

Davitt's first impression of John Boyle O'Reilly was given in a letter from Hartford, Conn., written about 1 October 1878, but dated simply 'Friday evening'. He had a fine meeting in Lawrence, Mass., and had stopped over in Boston on his way to Hartford, New Britain and New Haven. As usual, he had visited the private meetings everywhere he went. He writes:

> Saw fifty of the Lowell men with their President. Called on O'Reilly in Boston. I am disappointed in him. He hopes we (the Irish) will never become conspirators. This came out of a discussion of home affairs. I told him I did not like his article on the Fund in this week's *Pilot*. Read it. O'Kelly is in Boston and he promises to talk to him about writing of the Fund in such a 'damning by faint praise' style.
>
> Called on L—[1] *in re* H—,[2] the swindler. I don't care for L—. He talks of H— and his robbery as if it was an unimportant affair. He evidently knows where he is and promises to look him up. I suggested to old Cannon that it would be well to send home to Bradford the amount H— paid back. If sent through the Doctor it will encourage the efforts McG—[3] is now making to start work there again.

I will not reach New York before Monday afternoon.
    Fraternally yours,
    Michael

Have met crowds of North of England fellows – all working well.

Davitt in this letter throws his keen anxiety to recover the amount of a defalcation committed by a man who had absconded from the North of England and whose name was in a 'black list' sent to us by the men at home. He leaves no doubt as to his wish in this matter. He wanted the defaulter to make good, for the effect it would have in reorganising Bradford. Davitt was a Fenian then and wanted to see organised Fenianism flourish at home and abroad. He located two or three other defaulters from the North of England and they were either made to disgorge or forced to decamp.

In a letter dated 'Manayunk, Saturday', and evidently from allusions to recent events which cannot be quoted here, written shortly before he sailed for Ireland, Davitt says:

> I wish I was back again. I am told that there is a split between Parnell, Biggar[4] and Power. Biggar has told my informant. . . .
>
> I am sure you are delighted with the Belfast fellows for the lesson they taught Sir Eye-Glass. G— has smashed him in his letter to the *Freeman*. . . .
>
> I wish you were by the Seine, myself at home again and our paper started.

At this time we were talking of starting a Nationalist weekly paper in Dublin to get rid of Richard Pigott, and Davitt had a hobby that I could direct it from Paris, as I could not then live in Ireland, the terms of my release from prison exiling me until the expiration on 10 February 1882, of my fifteen years' sentence. I had told him that the idea of a man editing a Dublin paper from Paris was absurd, that proper editing could only be done in the office of the paper, but it took a long time to get the idea out of his head. This subject of the paper will come up again, as Pigott's financial dishonesty – and political depravity made his control of the Dublin *Irishman* a constant menace.

There were many short letters and telegrams after Davitt went West of Cleveland, but there was nothing important in them. Those from St Louis and other parts of Missouri were mainly concerned with the disappointment and fatigue caused by the bad management of that part of the tour by a man who has been dead for many years.

From Dubuque, Iowa, he wrote a long and most interesting letter which I give in full:

Dubuque, 31 October, 1878

MY DEAR DEVOY – Owing to the rivalry of two local papers in this city who are catering for Irish support, your unfortunate humble servant has been the topic of topics since his arrival here. My lecture in Globe Hall last night was fairly attended – large numbers of Americans being present. The aforesaid couple of sheets are attacking each other for 'slurs' cast upon myself in particular and everything Irish besides, and the whole town is by the ears. The Mayor and all the Corporation have taken sides with us, and we have carried the situation. The *Herald* (the enemy) has come out this morning with a 'tremendous'; complimentary notice of my lecture, and quoted the *Times* (the friendly organ) as making disparaging allusions a few days ago. All this is lively, but awfully annoying.

I visited the clubs in St Louis, Sedalla, Marshall, Hannibal, Ottumwa, and this city, since I wrote to you after seeing the Chicago men. I am sorry I cannot see more of those splendid Western fellows. What a field there is out here for work in our movement. Owing to the fact that some projected lectures are abandoned and that the few delivered will not defray the expense, I have to relinquish my intention of going to Omaha and Denver. These people out here believed that my only object was to make money, and they frankly tell me that lecturing won't do it. Had they been posted on my real desire (to see the Clan) they would have met me half way by endeavouring to defray expenses in doing their best to make lectures meet the cost of travel. As it is, they have attempted to do nothing, under the impression that *more* was required than they could accomplish.

I am leaving for St Paul tomorrow morning. If the proceeds of two lectures to be delivered in that neighbourhood will enable me to go to Omaha, I will visit the club there and call in Sioux City *en route* –. If not, I must turn back.

I have had a letter from O'Kelly telling me that if our people in Boston co-operated with O'Reilly and Joyce a lecture in that city could be made a success. I have written to the Doctor on the matter and leave it in his hands. As my expenses out here have been devilish heavy I fear I must go on the stump in the East again to take myself and mother home.

O'Kelly tells me that he does not intend returning to New York. I am of opinion that if he was asked by the C. G.[Clan na Gael] to go to Ireland, he would do so. . . . As I am certain that when Mahon, the Doctor and yourself meet, you will be required to proceed to Paris to direct the paper from thence, it is of consequence to know who would be best qualified to *superintend* the paper in Dublin and act as your deputy there on its staff.

I don't know anyone in the range of my acquaintance so qualified for this work as O'Kelly. He shares our ideas in everything excepting a more charitable opinion of O'Donnell and Power. There would be no fear of that opinion operating against the policy of C. G. in the new organ, for I am confident he would act within the lines of that policy when instructed and required to do so. He has a good record at home, and his connection with our paper would be certain to give satisfaction. His knowledge of military matters would dispense with the sending of M— or any other such authority to the other side for some time to come. Taken altogether, I think no more suitable man could be found for the work to be done, and it ought to be our particular desire now to wheel every *thinking* and *earnest* man of our movement into positions where they can do most good. I hope you will think this matter over pending the meeting between yourself and your two colleagues and I am assured you will see the advantage of having such a man in such a position. I have written to the Dr on the same subject.

I hope to be back East in about a fortnight or three weeks' time.

Yours ever sincerely,
Michael

The omitted portions of the above letter marked by asterisks refer to matters of a personal character. The references to Mr James O'Kelly's going over to the other side of the Atlantic might in the case of any other man now living under the authority of the British Government do some harm, but in this case they can do none. In Mr O'Kelly's evidence before the Parnell Commission he made a frank admission of the object of his mission to Ireland, taking full responsibility for it, but refusing to divulge the names of those who sent him or those to whom he was accredited, or any details whatever. The entire success of this line of action, the Commission having no power to compel him to answer, proved its wisdom and it is regrettable that the example was not followed by others. This matter will come up again in its proper place.

Davitt worked his way back eastward, delivering a few lectures as he came and attending the private meetings of the Clan. The lectures helped to make up for the losses incurred in the Western trip, and at all the private meetings Davitt pledged himself that the proposed public movement would not be used to hurt Fenianism, to decry Fenian ideals, but rather as a means of broadcasting the scope of Fenian activities and committing the mass of the people to a more advanced programme than that put forward by Isaac Butt's federal Home Rule movement.

These pledges were rendered necessary by misgivings expressed in letters from friends at home to men in America as to the scope and probable effect of the new movement. These misgivings were the direct result of the skilful misrepresentations of Richard Pigott in the *Irishman*. Davitt met them squarely by assuring the members that what he aimed at was a strong and aggressive public movement animated by the spirit of Fenianism and controlled by a combination between the Fenians and the more advanced section of the Home Rulers.

Abandonment of Fenianism, either in its organised form or its ultimate aims, he assured the men present at these private meetings, was entirely out of the question. And while he always insisted on the necessity of enlisting the farmers by making vigorous agitation of the Land Question a prominent feature of the proposed new movement, there was at that time no question whatever of starting a separate and distinct land agitation. That agitation was destined to come later through the distress of 1879 and the refusal of the Fenians at home to adopt the whole of the American programme. I say 'the whole' because it is not true that they rejected all of it, as will be seen later.

While Davitt was in Missouri and could not be reached by wire (about 24 October 1878), a cable despatch to the New York *Herald* reporting the proceedings of the Convention of the Home Rule Confederation of Great Britain, held in Dublin the day before, and at which Parnell was elected President, misled us into the belief that there was an open rupture between Parnell and Butt. When the full accounts reached us by mail, we saw our error, but the proceedings at that Convention none the less placed Parnell in the running for the leadership. The Home Rule Confederation of Great Britain was the English branch of Isaac Butt's Home Rule League. The *Herald's* foreign news was always wired to the leading papers all over the country and the publication of this misleading despatch aroused great interest among Irish Nationalists in America, who never had any faith in Butt's tame and halting policy.

Telegrams were hastily exchanged between the leading Clansmen in the United States and with some Nationalists of a milder type who were not in any organisation, and the result was that the following cablegram was sent on 25 October, to Charles J. Kickham for presentation to Parnell if Kickham approved.

Nationalists here will support you on the following conditions:

First – Abandonment of the federal demand and substitution of a general declaration in favour of Self-Government.

Second – Vigorous agitation of the Land Question on the basis of a peasant proprietary, while accepting concessions tending to abolish arbitrary eviction.

Third – Exclusion of all sectarian issues from the platform.

Fourth – Irish members to vote together on all Imperial and Home questions, adopt an aggressive policy and energetically resist coercive legislation.

Fifth – Advocacy of all struggling Nationalities in the British Empire and elsewhere.

This despatch was signed by Dr William Carroll of Philadelphia, John J. Breslin, F. F. Millen[5] and John Devoy of New York, and Patrick Mahon of Rochester N.Y. It was published in the New York *Herald* next day. On 27 October the *Herald* published a series of interviews with prominent

Nationalists, including Thomas Clarke Luby,[6] Colonel Thomas Francis Bourke[7] and John J. Breslin. The interviews were written by me and submitted before publication to the persons whose names were used. I wrote the heading, the first line of which was 'An Irish New Departure', and the same term was used in the introduction. In the discussions which followed the same term was used to describe the policy proposed and that was how the movement at that stage happened to be called by that name.

As the proposition was not made in the name of any organisation, and several men who were not members of the Clan had pledged their support to it, and it contemplated only work in public, it is hardly correct to say that it was 'conspiring in public'. It did not ask Parnell to commit himself either to the Fenians in Ireland or to the Clan na Gael in America, but to a public programme which all Irishmen who approved of it could publicly support. It was sent to Kickham,[8] rather than direct to Parnell, at the request of Dr Carroll of Philadelphia, as an act of courtesy to the then head of the Fenians in Ireland and to give the proposition additional weight if he approved of it. It is not a matter of much public consequence now whether Parnell received the cablegram from Charles J. Kickham or not, as its publication made him fully acquainted with its contents. This I know, that Kickham told me later on that he sent it to Parnell by mail with a short letter stating that he did not approve of the proposition but forwarded it because the senders had requested him to do so. In my talks with Parnell a few months later I did not bother asking him whether he had received the cable or not, because his familiarity with the contents of the message and with the discussion which its publication had brought forth made it wholly unnecessary.

As twenty-eight years have elapsed since then the political conditions which led up to this action are only understood by the few now living who were actively engaged in the National Movement at the time. A brief explanation may therefore be in order.

*

Isaac Butt's Home Rule Movement was not, properly speaking, a federal one, and the term was only used in the cablegram because it was so described at the time by Butt himself. Butt's idea of Home Rule was the creation by an act of the British Parliament, of a subordinate legislative body in Ireland whose powers would be defined by the act which, of course, would be subject to amendment or revocation at the will of the supreme authority which had called it into existence.

Butt was liked personally by the Fenians for his splendid defence of the men in the dock and for his active part, with George Henry Moore[9] and John Nolan,[10] in the Amnesty Movement which had secured the release of all of the convicted men except the military Fenians and those sentenced for participation in the Manchester Rescue.[11] But the great majority of the Fenians at home and all of them in America regarded his Home Rule plan as a surrender of Ireland's right and believed that the propaganda in its favour was calculated to undermine the principle of Nationality. A few active Fenians, mostly in the North of England, and many ex-members in Ireland, supported Butt, and their action led to much friction inside the ranks of Fenianism. Davitt was on very friendly terms with all these 'Home Rulers and Something More' and pleaded hard with us to devise some means by which a common ground of action for them and us could be afforded. The first plank in the cabled programme was intended to accomplish this.

Butt's efforts in the direction of the Land Question were for securing 'the three Fs', meaning 'Fixity of Tenure, Fair Rents and Free Sale,' which would settle nothing. The second plank aimed at educating the people up to a more radical land settlement which could really only be effected by an independent Ireland.

The third plank, 'Exclusion of all sectarian issues from the platform' was aimed at the rotten politicians – lawyers, country squires and shoneens – who really controlled Butt and who sought election to Parliament by swallowing every pledge they were asked to make and forgot them after election, and also at the Whig[12] bishops and priests who helped to get these fellows elected. Poor as Butt's programme was, it was not on that platform that Members of Parliament were elected, but on a hodge-podge which included many other things. The candidate pledged himself to 'Home Rule, Tenant Right, Catholic Education and the Restoration of the Temporal Power of the Pope', with his tongue in his cheek, and did nothing at all when he got to London. So long as this practice continued it was idle to expect the co-operation of the mass of Irish Protestants. It was hard enough to get them under any circumstances, but this programme repelled them. Hence 'the exclusion of sectarian issues' was demanded.

The fourth plank requiring Irish Members to 'vote together on all Imperial and Home questions' was intended to create an independent party whose action would attract foreign attention and be ready to withdraw from the British Parliament and meet in Dublin when the time should be ripe.

The fifth plank was intended to create a bond of sympathy and prepare the way for future co-operation between the Irish and other peoples, who, like the Boers and the Indians, were suffering at the hands of the common enemy.

That this was the meaning of the 'New Departure' cablegram, instead of what Richard Pigott described it in the *Irishman* – an abandonment of Fenianism, will be clearly shown by the interviews on the subject published in the New York *Herald* of 27 October 1878, and immediately printed in pamphlet form and circulated among the Nationalists of the United States, which I will reprint next week. This publication was, together with the cablegram, the subject of discussion at conferences attended by Davitt before his departure for Ireland, in December 1878, again, with the addition of a letter subsequently written to the Dublin *Freeman* at a meeting in Paris and again at a two days' conference with Parnell and Biggar at Boulogne, France, before I reached Ireland in the early part of 1879. I am in a position to prove all this, and, as no living man can be hurt by it and the interests of the Irish cause demand it, I propose to publish the whole story, suppressing such portions only as deal with revolutionary work or affect men still at the mercy of the British Government.

Chapter 5

Michael Davitt and the Clan na Gael

Following the 'New Departure' cablegram to Mr Parnell and the explanation of the propositions contained in it, which I gave last week, it is proper that I should give the views of some of the well-known men in America who approved of the policy, as they were published at the time. The interviews with these gentlemen were not only published in the New York *Herald* within a day or two after the sending of the cablegram to Parnell, but were printed in pamphlet form and sent to every branch of the Clan na Gael in the United States, as well as to a number of men who belonged to no organisation at all. This circulation put the stamp of official approval on the scheme, so far as the Clan was concerned, and left no room for doubt as to how the proposition was to be understood. This understanding must be taken into account. The interviews will be found below.

NEW DEPARTURE EXPLAINED

(From New York *Herald*, 27 Oct. 1878)

The Home Rule Conference in Dublin, the result of which was chronicled in the special cable despatch from that city, published in the *Herald* of Thursday, together with the action taken thereon by the Irish Nationalists of the United States, as reported in Friday's *Herald*, is the subject of much comment among the Irish population, and it is thought that the next few weeks will see a veritable 'new departure' in Irish National politics.

The change, it is said by those competent to speak on the subject, will take the shape of a combination between the advocates of physical force and those who believe in constitutional agitation, such as will leave the former free to prepare for active work while, in the meantime, giving a reasonable support to a dignified and manly demand for Self-Government on the part of the Constitutionalists.

It has been felt for a long time by the more thoughtful of the extreme Nationalist leaders that a mere conspiracy would never achieve their ends and that a public policy was necessary, so that the voice of the majority might prevail in Ireland and a real public opinion be developed in the country. They claim that the Separatist party is in the immense majority and that it is only the policy of abstention from public life and the avoidance of constitutional agitation which gives the apparent majority to those who favour connection with England in any form.

'A new departure is necessary,' said a prominent Nationalist to a *Herald* reporter yesterday,

> if we are ever to be properly understood by the world, and especially by that portion of it which is inimical to England. We must secure the control of the public voice of the country by electing men to Parliament and to the local municipal bodies who will not misrepresent us. We have never been properly represented, simply because since the passage of the Ballot Act – for before that it was impossible – we have abstained from interference in elections, except on particular occasions – such as the elections of O'Donovan Rossa[1] and John Mitchel[2] for Tipperary – and in these instances we demonstrated what we could do.
>
> Now, Ireland can never be freed through the British Parliament, or by constitutional agitation in any form, but constitutional agitation is one means of advancing our cause and we should avail ourselves of it. The world judges us – and, above all, England's enemies judge us – by our public representatives, and in the times that are coming we cannot afford to be misrepresented any longer. There is no use sending men to the British Parliament to beg, but we can send men there to protest before the world against England's right to govern Ireland, and when all is ripe we can command our representatives to withdraw from the

British Parliament and meet in Ireland as an Irish Legislature. It is only through such means that the whole Irish race the world over can be aroused and their active sympathy enlisted, and when that occurs I claim that the work is half done and we can wait patiently for the result.

'Do the Irish Nationalists intend to abandon their physical force theories and mainly depend on constitutional agitation?' asked the *Herald* reporter.

Not by any means. We simply don't believe in little insurrections that England can crush in a few days or weeks. We propose that, in the event of war, Ireland shall keep quiet, at least for a time, and simply formulate her just demands that the organised Nationalists outside of Ireland shall actively assist England's enemies and hurt her wherever they can. They can do this to an extent that is little thought of now. This is our pro-gramme – peace at home, active aggression against England wherever a blow can be delivered to the best advantage. This is all I can tell you just now, and there is no use asking me any more about it.

'To what extent do you and your friends propose to support the active section of the Home Rulers led by Mr Parnell?'

We won't support them at all, except they give up their sham federal programme and exclude sectarianism from their policy. We don't propose, for instance, to turn over the education of the rising generation to the Catholic hierarchy, many of whom are the bitterest enemies of an independent Irish nationality. We want a sound national education for all creeds and classes, and we want to leave the Pope to settle his political differences with Italy without our interference. However, on these points we shall be satisfied to support men who differ with us if their theories are left out of the platform which binds the party together, provided they agree with us on essential points.

There are more pressing questions to be settled than the Education Question. The Land Question is the vital one in Ireland and demands immediate attention. Our grievance with regard to the present so-called

'National' system of education is that, while the teaching is really very good, it is not national in any sense of the word, but the Bishops offer us nothing better. The Catholic University wasted the people's money on illuminations for the Prince of Wales and gives its best professorships to English Catholics; and, besides, many of the Bishops are the persistent enemies of the National cause.

If they were with the people on the National Question we might be disposed to support them, but we don't propose to make the Irish Nationalist Movement an engine for the conversion of England to Catholicism. The Church can do its own work through its own machinery, and we don't care whether English rule in Ireland is Catholic or Protestant, we want to put an end to it. We do not propose to oppose those who support the Bishops: we simply object to have their education or other demands tacked on to the National platform.

'Have you seen the copy of the cable despatch sent to Dublin and published in Friday's *Herald*?'

Certainly. The conditions therein named are the only ones on which the advanced Nationalists here will support Mr Parnell and his friends. They are very reasonable and I think they will be accepted. We consider that if Parnell and his friends accept these terms a new era dawns for the Irish National Party, and that the next election will give us some fifty earnest representatives, and some thirty or forty more who will vote with them to keep their seats. In any case, Butt's leadership is a thing of the past and his mongrel 'federal' scheme has fallen to the ground. If Parnell does not accept: we can do without him, but not so well. He is a very good man and means well to Ireland. All of us respect him, but have no faith in O'Donnell.[3]

'What are the prospects of the Irish National Party?'

It is now a thoroughly united party the world over: and a union such as we propose with the advanced Home Rulers would enable us to accomplish much. If it is effected, look out for stirring times.

Mr Thomas Clarke Luby, formerly editor of the Dublin *Irish People* and author of several Irish historical works, was next visited. Mr Luby said he had a very high opinion of Mr Parnell personally, and hoped to see his opinions ripen in time, but he had never had any faith in Mr Butt's federal scheme. He had considerable reserve in favouring any connections with Parliamentary politics, but thought that on the conditions proposed by the Nationalists, if the Parnell wing of the Home Rulers would give guarantees, it would be safe to come to an understanding. 'I believe with other Nationalists,' said Mr Luby,

> that a mere conspiracy will never accomplish our work. We must create a sound public opinion in Ireland and we can't afford to be misrepresented. It would be an immense gain if we could control the Parliamentary representations and the local public bodies – but we should exact guarantees. With our experience of Parliamentary agitation we should be very careful in dealing with it.

'Some of your Nationalist friends, Mr Luby, have an idea that if a majority of the Members of Parliament were secured, and the country were otherwise ready, they could meet in Ireland and declare themselves an Irish Legislature, the Nationalists making that declaration the signal for a war of independence. Would you be in favour of such a policy?'

> Certainly. If such a state of things could be brought about, especially if England were engaged in war, it would be the proper thing to do and the best means of enlisting the active sympathy and co-operation of the whole Irish race. It would also give us a standing before the world that mere insurrection would never give us.

Mr John J. Breslin, the rescuer of the Australian prisoners,[4] was called upon for the purpose of ascertaining his views in relation to the proposed alliance with the Home Rulers. As he is also the man who released James Stephens from Richmond Prison, his opinion on the question of Stephens is worth considering, and he gave it to the *Herald* reporter without the slightest hesitation.

I am entirely in favour of the proposition forwarded to Mr Parnell by cable, and I think it is necessary to prevent Ireland from being misrepresented before the world by men who claim to speak in the name of the country. I would like to see a union effected between the advanced Nationalists and the more earnest of the Home Rulers for this purpose, and I consider it is only by such a union we can defeat those who now misrepresent Ireland. I have the utmost confidence in Mr Parnell's honesty of purpose, and I hope to see the proposed union effected. At the same time I think the Irish Nationalists here should not relax their preparations for active work for one moment; for it is by active, aggressive work alone we can ultimately succeed.

On this subject Mr Breslin's views were substantially the same as those given expression to by other gentlemen visited.

'I am,' said Thomas F. Bourke,[5]

decidedly in favour of the proposed alliance with Mr Parnell and the active section of the Home Rulers, and think much good can be accomplished by it. At the same time I believe now, as I have ever believed, that nothing but force can ever free Ireland. Before that day comes, however, here is much to be done; and I think it would be sheer folly to throw away whatever chance of doing good may be offered by constitutional action. I have every confidence in Mr Parnell, but have no faith in Mr Butt's so-called 'federal' scheme.

Several other prominent Irish Nationalists were also visited, but the opinions expressed were the same in substance as those given above. The *Herald* reporter found everywhere a desire to unite with the advanced Home Rulers, if they would discard Mr Butt's federal programme, act together on all questions, and grapple with the land question in a thoroughly practical manner. The feeling against Irish landlordism the reporter found to be very intense, and a desire almost universally expressed that the whole system should be swept away; at the same time that much was said in praise of certain individual members of the landlord class.

Fenianism, as people will persist in calling the extreme form of Irish Nationality, seems really to be about to take a 'new departure', and to be destined to play a more active part in the public life of Ireland than at any previous time. The reporter was assured that lively times are ahead in both England and Ireland, which will act as a strong stimulant on the Irish movement in America, and create no small excitement. The belief in mere isolated insurrectionary movements seems to have died out, and to be replaced by a determination to obtain such a public standing in Ireland as will attract the attention of the world, and secure alliances with England's enemies.

Davitt, as soon as he read the news of the sending of the cablegram, was alarmed lest its publication should frighten some of the 'moderate' people in Ireland who were never disposed to support Parnell. He wrote a hurried letter saying as much and when he returned to New York he was of the same mind. He did not disapprove of any of the propositions, but simply feared the effect of their publication and doubted that Parnell would accept them all. We thrashed the matter out with him, allayed his fears and convinced him that boldness was the best policy in a matter of this kind and that the sooner public discussion was forced on the merits of the proposition the better.

The two principal things that occurred between the publication of these interviews and Davitt's departure for Ireland were a meeting of the governing body of the Clan na Gael, which Davitt attended, and a conference with John Boyle O'Reilly and Dr Robert Dwyer Joyce. At both of these meetings this public pronouncement was the basis of discussion, and at the Clan meeting the complexion which it put on the 'New Departure' was approved. It was distinctly on Davitt's acceptance of this interpretation that support was promised him and that I was requested to go to the other side of the Atlantic to help Davitt, as well as to perform other duties, which need not be mentioned here. If Davitt had not agreed to that interpretation the Clan would not have promised him its support and I would not have crossed the Atlantic to help him.

Chapter 6

Returned to Ireland to open campaign

After Davitt's return to the East and about a week before his Boston lecture (which was held on 8 December 1878) there was a meeting of the governing body of the Clan na Gael in New York,[1] to which he was invited. The invitation was extended to him because he was a member of the governing body of the Fenian organisation at home. His advice was wanted in regard to our relations with our brethren at the other side of the Atlantic, and it was necessary to have a clear and definite understanding with him in regard to the proposed public movement. Davitt was present during the whole of the proceedings, although much of the business transacted had no concern with anything but the routine work of the organisation.

Davitt's misgivings as to the effect of the publication of the cablegram on the 'moderate' people in Ireland had already been allayed and no time was wasted in discussing that aspect of it. But Richard Pigott was waging a relentless warfare on the 'New Departure' and his paper, the *Irishman*, being largely read by the Fenians at home, very many of them were led to take Pigott's view of it. These were mainly men of limited education, but the educated men who were the leaders of Fenianism were opposed to the 'New Departure' because it seemed to them to be either an abandonment of the Fenian policy or likely to lead to a mere Parliamentary agitation, bound to end, as all such movement had ended in the past, in failure and possibly worse.

Letters from both of these classes of men were appearing in the *Irishman* and Pigott adroitly fanned the flame of disapproval. Pigott's bread and butter was at stake. His policy was to pretend sympathy for the policy of abstention from public life and try to swing the Fenians into line for all Parliamentary candidates who paid him his price. One of his favourites was a Jew who thought that Pigott controlled 'the Nationalist vote', until convinced of his folly by much useless expenditure of money. If the Fenians should decide to take part in the public life of Ireland in a body and on lines clearly laid down Pigott's occupation would be gone, candidates could no longer be 'bled', and funds for Nationalist charities and testimonials would no longer be subscribed through the *Irishman* and misappropriated for Pigott's debaucheries.

It was this situation which troubled Davitt. He was about to go home and wanted all the help that we could give him. As there was perfect agreement between him and us, we were all anxious to do the best we could for him, for his own sake as well as for the good of the National Movement. The Clan's views were clearly set forth in the cablegram and the *Herald* interviews, and Davitt proposed to the body that I should be sent to the other side to help him to plead, first, with the Fenians for their acceptance, and, secondly with Parnell to induce him to accept the leadership of the new movement if it should be launched. These, and these only, were the things for which Davitt wanted me to cross the Atlantic. He broached the subject of a permanent residence in Paris and the starting of a paper in Dublin, but did not press them when I pointed out the impracticability. He only wanted me to go as far as Paris and did not expect me to visit Ireland.

I may be permitted to say here that I did not want to go to the other side at that time. The trip was very inconvenient to me. I was in the line of promotion on the *Herald*, a long absence meant the sacrifice of my prospects – and it turned out to be nearly ruinous. It was Davitt's strong pleading with me to stand by him in the bitter fight he saw before him that finally decided me, more than the request of my own colleagues, and I have since paid dearly for yielding. Dr Carroll had been over only a few months before, had satisfactorily settled our relations with the men at home, had seen Parnell (whom he had previously met in America in 1875) and had prepared the way for an understanding with him. There was, therefore, no necessity for sending another envoy, except that created by the publication of the new programme.

I agreed to go, got 'leave of absence without pay' from the *Herald*, and in a few days started with Davitt for Boston for a conference with O'Reilly, Joyce and Collins, who, however, was not able to be present. We were authorised to inform them that the Clan had agreed to the programme and that it was to that programme, as outlined in the cablegram to Parnell and in the *Herald* interviews that O'Reilly and Joyce gave their approval. Their only disappointment was when I explained to them that the fight in which both were getting ready to take part, was still some years ahead. O'Reilly hoped to become a dashing cavalry leader, while Joyce had elaborate schemes for casting guns to be mounted on cart axles, and for improvising powder factories, all of which he had carefully studied out. He assured us that he was familiar with almost every corner of Ireland, that every description of scenery in 'Deirdre'[2] had been written from actual observation, and that he had even swam rivers to satisfy himself that they could be crossed at certain points.

The Dublin *Freeman* had criticised the proposals from a different standpoint to that of either the home Fenians or Pigott. It considered the programme wild and impracticable, and I had written a short letter pointing out the errors of the article and asking space for a future letter answering all the criticisms. I made a rough draft of this second letter, submitted it to Davitt, to Dr Carroll, Patrick Mahon, of Rochester N. Y, to O'Reilly, Dr Joyce, P. A. Collins, Thomas Clarke Luby, James J. O'Kelly, Joseph I. C. Clarke, John J. Breslin and many others, and made alterations on the advice given me. I intended it, not as a presentation of my own views, but so far as possible to make it crystallise those of all the best thinkers in the National Movement in America. In the cabin of the French line steamer *Canada* I rewrote and rearranged the whole thing, dated it from New York and forwarded it from Paris to the *Freeman* through a German engineer from New Orleans, who informed the paper that he had promised to deliver it, but had been obliged to go by way of France and therefore sent it by mail. This was to conceal the fact that I had crossed the Atlantic.

I sailed for Havre on 11 December 1878 as before stated and Davitt took the *Cunarder* for Queenstown on the following day. As the letter to the *Freeman* mailed from Paris was the subject of prolonged discussion, largely due to a very dishonest summary of it published by Pigott in the *Irishman*, in which the omitted portions were malignantly misdescribed, it is proper that I should quote it in full here.

THAT FREEMAN LETTER

The Document Which Richard Pigott Mutilated
to Deceive Irish Nationalists

New York, 11 December 1878

To the Editor of the *Freeman*:

SIR – The frequent mention made of my name in the Irish press in connection with the so-called 'New Departure' proposed by a portion of the Irish National Party and the very serious errors which have been committed in interpreting the scope and meaning of that proposition, must be my excuse for obtruding myself on the attention of the Irish public. As the *Freeman* has published so much in connection with this controversy, I hope you will enable me to state the case from the standpoint of those responsible for the original proposition.

The question whether the advanced Irish National Party – the party of Separation – should continue the policy of isolation from the public life of the country which was inaugurated some twenty years ago by James Stephens and his associates – or return to older methods – methods as old, at least, as the days of the United Irishmen – is agitating the minds of Irish Nationalists on both sides of the Atlantic just now, and certainly no small incident has aroused such wide discussion in Ireland for many a day, as the publication of the views of the exiled Nationalists resident in New York on the subject. This shows conclusively the importance of the action proposed.

All intelligent Irishmen feel that the entrance in the everyday political life of the country of a large class of men with strong opinions and habits of organisation, but, who have hitherto held aloof from it, or only acted on rare occasions when a principle was considered at stake, would be an event that would largely influence the future of Ireland.

The eagerness with which the subject has been discussed by all persons would prove this if it were not otherwise sufficiently evident; but as might be expected, much difference of opinion exists as to the direction that future will take.

Almost every newspaper which treated this subject, almost every man who has expressed his opinion, has done so from a purely partisan standpoint. There have, it is true, been some notable exceptions, and on the whole, the reception of the proposal has been encouraging to the proposers.

As it is a question of public policy, to be carried out, if adopted, with in the limits of existing law, it can bear the fullest discussion. In fact, the more it is criticised the better, provided the criticisms be based upon actual facts – the propositions made and the view expressed by the proposers – not on data supplied by the fancy of the critics, or phantoms of sinister motives conjured up by diseased imaginations. Fair and free discussions of the public policy proposed for the acceptance of the National Party by men who certainly have a right to their opinions and some claim to a voice in the decision, fair and free discussion of their motives in proposing it, as one of those responsible, I am prepared to meet in a frank and friendly way.

To those who resort to misrepresentation and insinuation of unworthy motives, I will only say that my motives are sufficiently known to my fellow workers, and I do not propose to defend them. They will bear comparison with those of some who have been rather hasty in resorting to personalities. The policy proposed must stand or fall on its own merits. I would remind some of my 'Nationalist' critics, however, that misrepresentation on the part of men who live by scribbling cheap treason and who never stir a finger to do any real service to the cause for which they profess such zeal may, if persevered in, provoke a retaliation that would be somewhat inconvenient to them, and not at all edifying. This is all the notice I propose to take just now of the 'consistent' patriots who pen the twaddle about 'Fenians in Parliament', and the silly impertinence about 'American babble'.

That the discussion aroused on both sides of the Atlantic by the proposal of a 'New Departure' has done good, I am prepared to admit, but so many mistakes have been made on your side of the water and such an amount of misrepresentation indulged in, that a clearer explanation of the objects sought to be attained and the principles professed by the proposers is necessary to enable the Irish people to form a correct judgment on the question. I am convinced that on the judgment formed on this question by the Irish people, and on the action that judgement will dictate, depends Ireland's political future for many years to come.

Even at the risk of having merely ambitious motives attributed to me, I am determined that some recent utterances of mine on the subject of Parliamentary and Municipal representation and on the Land Question, which have been rather freely commented upon, shall be fully understood, at least by those who care to understand them, so that they may not be made the excuse for preventing action approved of in theory by the majority of Irish Nationalists, but not carried into effect through fear of affording help to a certain class of trading politicians. These politicians, it is feared, might succeed in turning the National Party into a mere machine for their own advancement, if the 'New Departure' were adopted, or if any other public policy were determined upon.

I am as much opposed to allowing the National Party to be used by worthless aspirants for Parliamentary honours as I am to see it made an instrument for the circulation of the nauseating cant about Nationality served up by trading speculators calling themselves 'National' newspapers, or that its only public appearance should be when called to applaud the bunkum of 'orators' who keep their tongues and their hands rather quiet when times of danger come. There is intelligence enough in the National Party to save it from the Parliamentary shams, just as it has intelligence enough to stamp as quacks and charlatans those who talk of fighting and sedulously avoid preparation for it. I am convinced that these fears of the Parliamentarians, where they are honestly entertained, are groundless now, while I fully admit there was ample excuse for them in the past.

The object aimed at by the advanced National Party – the recovery of Ireland's National Independence and the severance of all political connection with England – is one that would require the utmost efforts and the greatest sacrifices on the part of the whole Irish people. Unless the whole Irish people, or the great majority of them, undertake the task and lend their whole energies to its accomplishment – unless the best intellect – the financial resources, and the physical strength of the nation be enlisted in the effort, it can never be realised. Even with all these things in our favour the difficulties in our way would be enormous, but if firmly united and ably led, we could overcome them and the result achieved would be worth the sacrifices. I am not one of those who despair of Ireland's freedom, and am as much in favour of continuing the struggle today as some of those who talk louder against constitutional agitation.

I am convinced that the whole Irish people can be enlisted in an effort to free their native land and that they have within themselves the power to overcome all obstacles in their way. I feel satisfied that Ireland could maintain her existence as an independent nation, become a respectable power in Europe, provide comfortably for a large population within her borders and rival England in commerce and manufactures. I contend she can never attain the development to which her geographical position, her natural resources, and the moral and intellectual gifts of her people entitle her without becoming complete mistress of her own destinies and severing the connection with England. But I am also convinced that one section of the people alone can never win independence, and no political party, no matter how devoted or determined, can ever win the support of the whole people if they never come before the public and take part in the everyday life of the country.

I have often said it before, and I repeat it now again, that a mere conspiracy will never free Ireland. I am not arguing against conspiracy, but only pointing out the necessity of Irish Nationalists taking whatever public action for the advancement of the National cause they may find within their reach, such action as will place the aims and objects of the National Party in a more favourable light before the world and help to win the support of the whole Irish people.

Those who propose the 'New Departure' merely want to provide good wholesome work for the National Party which will have the effect of bringing all sections of Nationalists into closer relations by giving them a common ground to work upon; a platform really broad enough for all to stand upon, demanding no sacrifices of principle, no abandonment of Ireland's rights. The have long felt the necessity for some such action and imagine they can see in the present state of parties in Ireland the best opportunity for proposing it which has yet presented itself.

Some of the arguments used in favour of the policy of isolation are very plausible, some of them very absurd; but there is not one sufficiently strong to justify a continuance of it, under existing circumstances. When used by men who are, and have been for years, simply doing nothing, they do not deserve to be treated with common respect, as in the case of earnest men who practice what they preach. The proof that these arguments do not convince the people – not even the rank and file of Nationalists – is to be found in the incontrovertible fact that the great majority of those who believe in independence, and who have the franchise, vote at all elections.

Even if there were a 'traditional policy', a 'beaten path', some of us would take the liberty of going outside of one or the other, if by doing so we thought we could advance the National cause. For myself, I must plead guilty to a strong disinclination to walk in the narrow 'paths', or 'tracks', or 'grooves', marked out for my guidance by people whose ability for leadership, whose earnestness and whose judgement, I have the best reason to doubt. I yield to no man living in the lengths I am prepared to go to get rid of foreign domination in Ireland, but I refuse to be guided by the narrow dogmatism through the instrumentality of which a few pigmies [*sic*] managed for a sad decade or so, to retain a leadership for which neither nature nor training ever fitted them. I want to see the national will consulted through the only means at present available, and when the country speaks, I am not afraid of the result, for I am convinced that Ireland desires Independence today as ardently as ever, and that nothing less will ever satisfy her. But it is simply absurd to ask the Irish people to follow a dangerous political course with their eyes blind-folded and trusting implicitly in guides of whom they know nothing. I am willing to trust the people, and think the issue is safe in their hands. When the country is convinced of the necessity for vigorous and decided action, I am not one of those who think the responsibility will be shirked. It was not the people who failed in recent National movements, but those who, without the capacity, the judgment or the courage necessary to lead the people in times of trial and danger, assumed the responsibility and broke down when the ordeal came. The Irish people have had more than enough of this kind of thing, and want no more self-appointed leaders or men labouring under a hallucination that they were born with a mission to regenerate them.

The advanced National Party in Ireland has never had a clearly defined policy further than a declaration in favour of independence, or sometimes, an independent Republic, to be obtained by force of arms. The people have never been told the kind of an Ireland we should have if the making of it depended on the Nationalists or how the Nationalists proposed to grapple with any of the burning social and political questions which would demand solution if the country were freed tomorrow. The national sentiment of the people alone was appealed to, especially in the Fenian movement, while their judgment as to the capacity of the men who proposed to regenerate them was left entirely out of the question. Of course, the people had many opportunities of forming an opinion on these points through public speeches and writings, but in this respect the constitutional agitation, honest or dishonest, had many advantages over the extreme Nationalists, inasmuch as public profession of their principles or intentions brought the latter into conflict with the law. The lack of political training and of practical acquaintance with public business – such, even as could be acquired by membership of a Town Council – has always told heavily against the Nationalists, while their absence from such bodies left the whole country in the hands of the West Britons, who are only a miserable minority. This enabled the minority not alone to speak and act in the name of the country, but gave its members the means of strengthening and consolidating their party and crushing out their opponents. The more this is examined the more ruinous this policy of isolation will appear, and the more the advantage to be derived from an organised, steady and persistent effort to get possession of these local bodies will be seen. While I admit that the Nationalists now vote at these elections, I deny that they act as a body, or with any settled plan or purpose.

With the majority of these bodies in our possession, even without the Parliamentary representation, we should be in a position to do many things we can only dream of now. With the municipal bodies and men of spirit and determination as Parliamentary representatives, backed by the country and millions of the Irish race scattered over the world, there will be no necessity to go to London either to beg or to obstruct, and Irish Nationalists would have no more Tallaghts[3] or 'cabbage-gardens'[4] flung in their faces.

Can this be accomplished? I claim it can, but only by a combination between all sections of Irish Nationalists – between all those who are dissatisfied with the existing order of things and desire self-government in any form. The Home Rulers cannot do it, for no one among the people really believes in Mr Butt's so-called 'Federal' Scheme. The Nationalists cannot honestly support the scheme for it gives to the English Parliament the prerogative which belongs to the Irish people, of calling the proposed local Parliament into existence and defining its powers, therefore having the right to abolish it by a simple act. It is a concession of England's right to rule Ireland.

The Repealers[5] can never again arouse the enthusiasm of the people; because, though having a strong historical point in their favour, simple Repeal would restore the Irish House of Lords, which few in Ireland would endure now. The Repealers, furthermore, are not organised, and many of them, as well as many weak-kneed Nationalists, support the Home Rulers for want of something better. In fact, the whole rank and file of the Home Rule Party is composed of men who would prefer a larger measure of Self-Government if it could be obtained.

The Nationalists could only obtain control of the local bodies and of the Parliamentary representation by the adoption of such a broad and comprehensive public policy as would secure the support of that large class of Irishmen who now hold aloof from all parties but are Nationalists in heart and feeling, and vote for the man who come nearest to their ideas, and which would further detach from the Home Rule Party all who are really in favour of a larger demand than that of Mr Butt, but who now give the Home Rulers a conditional support.

The object, however, would be reached much more easily by an honourable compromise. This compromise is only possible by leaving the form of Self-Government undefined – putting off the definition until a really representative body, with the country at its back, and elected with that mandate, could be assembled and speak in the name of the nation. When the nation speaks, all parties must obey, and a united Irish nation can shape its own destiny. There is no use defining the form of Self-Government for the mere purpose of bringing forward a motion in Parliament once a year, or once every session, only to be thrown out by a hostile majority; and complete independence cannot be demanded without coming into conflict with the law. *As the battle of Irish freedom must be fought outside of Parliament*, and as the Home Rulers, Repealers and Nationalists, all call the form of autonomy they desire, 'Self-Government' – as, in addition to this, they agree substantially as to the present needs of Ireland, there should be nothing to prevent them agreeing on a common platform which would bind them together for the common good of the country, till the country itself should speak in such a manner as to command the allegiance of all.

Such a common platform was suggested in the cable despatch from New York, which has been called the 'New Departure'. The talk about the 'folly' of publishing the substance of this telegram is almost too silly to waste words upon. It is simply the height of folly to imagine there was anything to be concealed in it. There was nothing proposed which was not strictly within the law, and no man in Ireland would have the slightest reason to fear the consequences of his acceptance of the propositions.

They would not bind a Member of Parliament to accept the revolutionary policy, nor could he be held responsible for the acts or speeches of the proposers in the United States. They simply bind all who accept them to carry them out, and the carrying of them out breaks no English law. It is not an alliance between Home Rulers and Revolutionists, but the adoption of a broad and comprehensive public policy which Nationalists and men of more moderate views could alike support without sacrifice of principle.

No party, or combination of parties in Ireland, can ever hope to win the support of the majority of the people, except it honestly proposes *a radical reform of the land system.* No matter what may be said in favour of individual landlords, the whole system was founded on robbery and fraud, and has been perpetuated by cruelty, injustice, extortion, and hatred of the people. The men who got small farms in the times of confiscation settled down in the county, and their descendants, no matter what their political party, are now 'bone of our bone' – have become Irish – and perform a useful function in the land. No one thinks of disturbing them. If the landlords had become Irish, and treated the people with humanity, the original robbery might be forgiven – though a radical change in the tenure of land must come of itself some day: but when, as a class, they have simply done England's work of rooting out the Irish people; when the history of landlordism is simply a dark story of heartless cruelty, of artificial famines, of evictions, of rags and squalid misery, there is no reason why we should forget that the system was forced upon us by England, and that the majority of the present landlords are the inheritors of the robber horde sent over by Elizabeth and James I, by Cromwell and William of Orange, to garrison the country for England. It is the interest of Ireland that *the land should be owned by those who till the soil* and this should be reached without even inflicting hardships on those who deserve no leniency at the hands of the Irish people. A solution of the Land Question has been reached to a large extent in France, in Prussia and in Belgium by enabling the occupiers to purchase their holdings. Let the Irish landlords be given a last chance of settling the Irish Land Question amicably in this manner, or wait for a solution in which they shall have no part. Let a beginning be made with the absentees, the English lords, and the London companies who hold stolen land in Ireland, and there will be enough of work for some years to come. *Let evictions be stopped at all hazards*, and the rooting out process come to an end. But I shall be told, the English Parliament will never do any of these things. Then, I say, these things must only wait till an Irish Parliament can do them better; but, in the meantime, good work will have been done, sound principles inculcated, and the country aroused and organised.

To those who are alarmed at language like this, in regard to the Land Question, I would say: 'Look at France, at Prussia, and at Belgium and you will find that the secret of their prosperity lies in the number of tillers of the soil who own their holdings. Listen to the muttering of the coming storm *in England* and ask yourself what is going to become of the land monopoly after a few more years of commercial and manufacturing depression – a depression sure to continue, because the causes of it are on the increase. The English are a very practical and a very selfish people, and will not let any fine sentiment stand in the way when they think it is in their interest to redistribute the land. What, may I ask, would become of the Irish landlords – especially the rack-renting, evicting ones – in case of a social convulsion in England? It is a question which they themselves must decide within the next few years. With them, or without them, the question will be settled before long, and many who now think the foregoing assertions extravagant, will consider them very moderate indeed, by and by.

The education question is only approached at present, from a purely religious standpoint. There is no reason why it should not be treated also from a utilitarian point of view, not to speak of a national one. The curse of Ireland for several centuries past, after foreign rule – indeed, as a direct result of foreign rule – is sectarianism. It is the interest of the Irish people that the rising generation of all creeds should receive a sound practical training that will fit them for the battle of life, and enable them to compete with the young men of countries hitherto more favoured in that respect. The natural resources of Ireland will never be developed by men trained as the majority of the present generation have been. Why not insist on the history of Ireland being taught in all our schools, and on the nationalisation of the schools where the Protestants are trained? It cannot be expected that men trained up in anti-Irish ideas will make good Irishmen; nor can it be expected that any large number of Protestants will join any political party which devotes its principal efforts to a purely Catholic object. It is the fear of the Catholic majority more than the love of England which makes anti-Irish Irishmen of so many of our Protestant fellow-countrymen: and if they are ever to be won over to the National side some sacrifice must be made. He must be a dull Irishman indeed who will assert that their aid is not worth having; and anything that is worth having is worth paying for. The price in this case is the exclusion of all sectarian issues from the National platform. This would not produce any miraculous transformation. We must wait for results: but they are sure to come for the simple reason that it is for the material interests of the Protestants, as well as the Catholics, that Ireland should govern herself.

If Ireland were free now, one of the first things, after the Land Question, which would demand solution, would be that of County Government and the principle should be laid down in the National Programme. The whole people have an interest in the local, as well as the National administration, and should have the selection of a County Council or Board, having much the same powers as the Council-General of a French department.

The present abortion of County Government, called a Grand Jury, which enables the foreign garrison to look after its own interests at the expense of the people, will not, of course, be abolished by the English Parliament, though it may be tinkered; but its abolition should be demanded, and the principle of the people's right to do their own business through their elected representatives clearly enunciated.

While the right to the franchise of every man born on Irish soil, who has not forfeited his rights to citizenship by conviction of a crime against society, should be affirmed, the very least that should be demanded, at present, is the equalisation of the Irish franchise with that of England.

If a programme such as I have roughly sketched above, were adopted and vigorously carried out, its acceptance made the test for election to all offices in the gift of the electors, and the people thoroughly organised for its support, the country would soon throb with a vigorous and healthy life from end to end, and we should at last begin to see the dawn of our day of liberation.

It would give Ireland the materials out of which a National Government could be formed which would command the confidence of the Irish people at home and abroad, and the respect of foreign nations.

From the very outset it would seriously embarrass the diplomacy of England abroad, and, if carried out with firmness, resolution and judgment, it would make Ireland count for something in the world, even before she won self-government.

It has been objected to by some very well-meaning people that the publication and explanation of this programme is the avowal of designs that England will take good care to provide against, but a little reflection will convince any intelligent man that the first public step taken as a result of its adoption would clearly indicate the ultimate object. It would be as clear as the noon-day sun to English statesmen but England has entered on a career on which she cannot stop, and she can no longer treat us as in the past.

That vast agglomeration of hostile races and conflicting interests, scattered over the world, called the British Empire, has been held together up to the present by favourable circumstances which are disappearing day by day. It is filled with inflammable material within, and beset with powerful and watchful enemies without. It was constructed for commercial purposes alone, is conducted on merely commercial principles, and cannot stand a great strain. It cannot last, and the crash will come as sure as fate. It has passed the summit of its glory and its infamy, and is now on the descent which leads inevitably to ruin. It is our turn now. Our watchwords should be *patience, prudence, courage* and *sleepless vigilance.* Great events are coming upon us, and on the way we demean ourselves during the next few years, will depend whether we are to play a considerable part in those events, and build up a nation or sink in the ruins of one of the broken empires of the world.

No one who looks at the present condition of the East, who considers the inevitable effects of the policy inaugurated by the present Government of England, and the settled policy of Russia – no one who has any knowledge of the immense interests at stake – can seriously think that war on one of the largest scales ever witnessed can much longer be averted. In such a war the blood and treasure of Ireland would be poured out like water for the interests of a power which has robbed us of everything and rooted out and exterminated our people. Ireland would gain nothing by it. It is time to ask: 'Shall Ireland have something to say about this expenditure of her vital resources, and, it if is inevitable, can she find no better way to apply them?' This is a question which Home Rulers, as well as Nationalists, will be called upon to answer some of these days, and now is the time to make up their minds.

It was considerations like these which dictated the proposition of the 'New Departure', and this explanation is given so that the Nationalists of Ireland may not be misled by the misrepresentations and the mistakes which have appeared in print in reference to it. They have as yet come to no decision: and I hope when they do, it will be a wise one. They must, however, beware of those 'friends' of theirs, who raise the cry of 'Dictation from America'. No one in America wants to dictate to them, but these gentlemen must pardon me if I respectfully decline the honour of being classed as an American.

Respectfully yours,
John Devoy

Among the men who most fiercely denounced the 'New Departure' were some who are now, or were since that time, Members of Parliament. 'Long John O'Connor[6] and J. C. Flynn,[7] now active members of the Parliamentary Party, were the joint authors of the letter signed 'Lee', which was referred to in the letter to the *Freeman*, and P. J. Sheridan[8] and others who were later very active in the Land League, denounced it as tending to 'demoralise the country'. Hardly any of them had read the full text of the letter in the *Freeman*, but all had read Pigott's 'revised' version.

Isaac Butt, however, was under no misapprehension as to the object aimed at. Saunders' *News-Letter*,[9] an old-fashioned Dublin Tory paper, had experienced a change of heart and became a mild Home Rule organ, in which Butt occasionally wrote articles. An editorial undoubtedly written by Butt in the *News-Letter* (which had taken a new name that I forget) vigorously attacked the letter in the *Freeman*, and among other things said that 'in spite of its studied moderation, the spirit of the Revolution breathed through every line of the letter'. English journals of standing took the same view of it and I think it is hardly necessary after twenty-eight years to claim that Butt and the Englishmen came nearer to gauging the object and intent of the letter than those of my Nationalist friends who differed with me at the time.

My next chapters will deal with the meeting in Paris, in so far as the proceedings dealt with the 'New Departure' and with a two days' conference with Parnell and Biggar in Boulogne a short time after.

Chapter 7

Davitt meets the Fenian leaders in Paris

Davitt knew that he had a hot campaign to face on his arrival in Ireland, and our programme was mapped out to meet it before we sailed from New York. He was to see his friends in Dublin, ascertain the exact situation and come over to Paris for a conference with me at the first opportunity before the meeting which was to take place there about the middle of January. The friend on whom he placed most reliance was Thomas Brennan,[1] afterwards Secretary of the Land League, and he was very confident that the younger men among the Fenians could be easily won over.

Davitt at that time was very impetuous and he alternated between extreme hopefulness and an irritability at all opposition almost verging on pessimism. He had no doubt whatever that he was right, or that the country would be with him if the case were placed fairly before it, but he exaggerated the effects of Pigott's malignant misrepresentation and he developed a feeling akin to personal animosity towards those who attacked the 'New Departure'. Their motives were bad and they were all either hypocrites or fools. This frame of mind is very common in Irish controversies, except among the best educated of the race, but Davitt at that time, fresh from prison with his mind filled with, to him, new ideas and without any previous experience of a public controversy, was the most pronounced case of it that I had ever met.

I landed in Havre after a ten days' voyage, went to Paris and put up at the Hotel du Louvre[2] under my assumed name, so that a French fellow-passenger who lived in New York might identify me at the Credit Lyonnais to get a draft cashed. Then I moved to the Continental for a day to break my track and get letters, and on Christmas Day moved to the Hotel Des Missions Étrangères,[3] a cheap but nice little place in the Rue du Bac, patronised mainly by priests and poor aristocrats. Here I was to meet Davitt and I registered under my proper name. I had stopped there in 1861 when on my way to join the Foreign Legion, and the Pope's Irish Brigade had spent a night under its roof on their return after Spoleto, Castelfidardo and Ancona in 1860. The same family were still running it.

Davitt wrote me a couple of short letters about his experiences in Dublin and then on 9 January 1879, I received the following telegram. 'JOHN DIXON: Poste Restate, Paris: Your friend will reach Paris eight tonight. Chemin de Fer du Nord Station. WEBSTER, London.'

The 'tall, dark man with a large Websterian head', as the Philadelphia reporter had described him, arrived at the Northern Railroad Station on time and I brought him to the little hostelry in the Rue du Bac. He was in bad need of rest. His system had been run down by more than seven years of hardship and insufficient nourishment in prison and his strenuous American tour had worn him out. During his stay in America he had not touched a drop of any alcoholic beverage and he had a prejudice against it that was almost morbid. He feared to taste wine or beer lest he should become a drunkard, a fear which his subsequent life proved to be utterly groundless, but for the moment it dominated him. Dr Joyce had recommended him to take claret with his dinner, but he had rejected the advice. I succeeded in breaking down his prejudice by pointing out the sober, quiet French people, lay and clerical, in the hotel, who drank wine moderately twice a day with their meals and never touched it during the rest of the day. He finally agreed to give it a trial, his appetite immediately improved and one fortnight in Paris made a wonderful improvement in him.

A Fenian official arrived a few day after Davitt to make arrangements for the meeting. Davitt, having failed to win him over to the 'New Departure' after a few conversations, developed a strong prejudice against him which he ever afterwards retained.[4] The man really had an open mind, but he was a Fenian to the marrow of his bone, judged everything in Ireland by its effects on Fenianism and had an abiding belief that all constitutional agitators were humbugs or worse. But he had a clear head and he freely recognised that we were placed at a great disadvantage by the fact that all the municipal and other local bodies were in the hands of our enemies. He was perfectly willing to see these local bodies captured, but saw no prospect of our accomplishing much with the limited franchise then in existence. He made no allowance for possible conversions through a public propaganda of many men who had the right to vote and he had a lingering suspicion that Davitt was, perhaps unknown to himself, under the influence of O'Connor Power[5] and that behind the 'New Departure' was some scheme of the latter which would be sprung at the opportune moment with disastrous consequences. Davitt resented the assumption that he was under any man's influence, but it was apparent to me that there was some reason to fear that the other man's theory had a basis of foundation in fact. He did not accuse Davitt directly of being under Power's influence, but what he did say irritated him and from that day Davitt branded that man as a 'trimmer' and an enemy of his – a very rash and unjust conclusion which influenced much of Davitt's subsequent action.

The meeting assembled in due time in a little hotel in a short street running from near the Odeon Theatre to the Boulevard Saint Michel and most of those who attended stopped at the hotel. Meals were served to the party separately in a small room, so that there was not occasion to go out, and they were entirely free from observation. Careful examination of the premises and surroundings showed that no detectives, either French or British, were on watch but it is quite possible that one of the hotel employees might have been an agent of the French secret police; but if so, he certainly could have only reported that a group of English speaking men were meeting in the house.

I have no right to discuss the purely Fenian business transacted at that meeting or to mention the names of living men who were present.[6] I will state merely what occurred in regard to the 'New Departure' and mention only the names of those who are now dead. The 'New Departure' was by no means the chief business discussed, nor was it the principal object of the mission on which the Clan na Gael had sent me, but it certainly occupied more time and was much more fully discussed than all the other items of business combined. But the regular business was disposed of before the subject of the proposed public movement was broached, although in private conversation it had been much discussed before the meeting.

The men present were the supreme governing body of a strong and vigorous organisation and the average of intelligence was very high. There were among them professional, literary and business men, clerks and artisans, and there could be no question that they represented the fighting spirit of Ireland. If they decided definitely against the 'New Departure' it would have a poor chance for life; the only organised fighting force in Ireland would obey their orders and the Clan na Gael would withdraw its support. Any intelligent man looking back over events in Ireland for the twenty years that have elapsed since then can easily guess what the result of an adverse decision would have been. Every man present realised what was at stake, and none more keenly than Davitt.

It was a unique gathering of revolutionists. The Chairman was Charles J. Kickham, whose influence over the Fenians of that day was infinitely greater than that of Stephens over the men of 1865. Nine-tenths of the old Fenians had never seen Stephens or heard his voice, he was merely a mysterious chief whom they had implicitly obeyed because they had been sworn to do so and had been told stories of his wondrous prowess and ability by their local leaders. He was the embodiment of 'the Irish Republic now virtually established', to which they had sworn allegiance, but not one in a thousand of them even knew his name until his arrest and rescue from prison in November 1865, made it known to the world. But long before they had learned who Stephens really was, the Fenians all over Ireland had been chorusing Kickham's 'Rory of the Hill' or reciting 'Patrick Sheehan', while many an Irish girl was singing 'She Lived Beside the Anner'. Old Fletcher of Saltoun's axiom,[7] was fully illustrated in Kickham's case. He had, besides, suffered in prison and in the years immediately preceding that Paris meeting everyone in Ireland deserving to be called Irish had read his *Knocknagow* and *Sally Cavanagh*, as the succeeding generation has continued to read them. Kickham, in 1878, was not only the idol of the Fenians, but he was their real leader.

Poets and literary men are not often good revolutionists – if the term be applied only to the practical work of revolution, for they certainly sow the seed – and they are seldom good politicians, but Kickham had a singularly good political head and was gifted with exceptionally sound judgment. Shut out from personal communication with everyone but the few most intimate with him by an accident in boyhood which almost completely deprived him of sight and hearing, he was at a great disadvantage in obtaining knowledge of what was going on around him. I had seen him preside at a meeting in Dublin in 1865 when a certain historic American document was under discussion, but his sight and hearing were then much better than after his strength had been broken down by the refined cruelties of the British prison system, and he got on fairly well. In Paris everything had to be conveyed to him through the fingers of his left hand by the deaf and dumb alphabet. The proceedings were given to him in summarised form in this way and he was so quick to grasp the meaning that neither words nor sentences had ever to be completed. Then he talked and his talk showed that he was keeping in marvellously close touch with all that was going on. The loss of sight and hearing had sharpened his other faculties, and his habit of introspection made him quick to grasp the movements of another man's mind.

The discussion on the 'New Departure' was opened in an irregular way by a little passage at arms between Davitt and a couple of those present over the merits of O'Connor Power and his probable attitude towards the proposed new movement. We in America had been induced to organise a lecture tour for Power a few years before and had got paid for our pains by a covert attack on the principles of Fenianism in the Cooper Institute. 'If you want me,' said Power, 'to take up an advanced position from which I am to be driven by the first shot fired from the guns of the enemy, then I tell you you may go and do it yourself. I did so once but that was before my college days.' Power's 'college days' were spent in St Jarlath's[8] long after he had grown to manhood and his expenses were paid by lectures got up for him by the Fenians in England and Ireland, but he loved to remind his hearers of his superior academic training. That expression was interpreted as the forerunner of his forthcoming recantation of Fenianism, and at the Manchester Martyrs'[9] celebration held in the same hall a few weeks later, Power was denounced as a renegade by Luby, Bourke, Mulcahy and O'Donovan Rossa, and three-fourths of his projected lectures in America were stopped. For a time he was able to keep the North of England division of the organisation aloof from the main body, and the trouble was ended by his being driven out with some of his partisans.

This was what made his name a red rag to some of our friends at home and during most of the discussions in Paris it was O'Connor Power, rather than the 'New Departure', that occupied the attention of those present. Eventually the good sense of the majority prevailed over the somewhat heated attitude of two or three who seemed to have 'O'Connor Power on the brain'. But the stage of calm discussion was not reached until an incident had occurred that almost broke up the meeting and came very near proving disastrous to Davitt's hopes and mine.

In this case it was Kickham's physical disabilities which led to the trouble. The 'interpreter', during most of the proceedings, was the Secretary of the meeting, who was an expert at conveying over Kickham's fingers what was going on and who acted with strict impartiality. Occasionally another, not so practiced in talking with his fingers, would do a little in that line after conveying his own views. As this got matters a little 'mixed' sometimes it became inconvenient to me and I learned to talk to Kickham in one evening's practice. When he closed his left hand that shut off the operator, who had to wait till he was done talking and held out his open left hand again. Attempting to reach him by talking on one's own hands was useless, for he could not see a single sign made. Davitt was handicapped by having only his left arm with which to reach Kickham's left hand and he gave up the attempt in disgust after a short trial. Indeed, he showed a distaste for it from the first and in his private talks with me was very sarcastic over making the fate of Ireland dependent on the impression conveyed to a physically helpless man through the deaf and dumb alphabet. Kickham instinctively felt that this was Davitt's attitude, and, finally, when the operator's opinion was conveyed along with the summary of a statement, he assumed that both were one, and made an indignant protest against 'dictation from America', based wholly on his misunderstanding of what had occurred.

As he had 'shut off the current' by closing his left hand there was no remedy until the connection could be made.

But before that could be done 'the gentle Charles' waxed more and more wrathful and said some things which were personally hurtful to Davitt, though not couched in offensive language, and other things which were unjust to the American organisation and which I could not let pass without protest. Others supported Kickham's stand with more zeal than discretion, the discussion became warm without ceasing to be in decorous language, and the reporting of proceedings to Kickham entirely ceased, leaving him still in ignorance of his error.

At last Davitt stood up, burst into a passionate flood of tears and announced between his sobs that he would withdraw from the meeting. Some of those present tried to dissuade him, telling him it was all a misunderstanding, but their pleadings were of no avail. He insisted on going, took his overcoat and hat and strode out of the room. I had made a vain attempt to convey to Kickham that he was labouring under a mistake, but 'the wires were down' and I could not reach him. Very much mortified and humiliated I saw that nothing could be done while Kickham remained in that frame of mind, so I withdrew with Davitt. It was then midnight and there was nobody around but ourselves.

We walked together through the Rue du Luxembourg to the Rue du Bac and Davitt sobbed bitterly most of the way, protesting indignantly against his treatment and insisting that Kickham intended deliberately to insult him. He only calmed down just as we reached the Hotel Des Missions Étrangères, where we both stayed, but we sat up a large part of the night discussing the incident. He was very despondent and saw no way out of the difficulty, the fancied insult to himself being the chief feature of it. He slept badly that night and looked haggard and weary the next morning. Early that morning the Secretary of the meeting called and brought a letter to me from one of the most respected members of the meeting asking that we come back that day. He was not a partisan of the 'New Departure', but favoured some portions of it which he wished to have calmly discussed, and he saw no good reason for our breaking away. He had great influence with Kickham and had fully explained to him during the evening the mistake under which he laboured.

After a talk with this gentleman and the Secretary, during which the positions of both sides were explained and a *modus vivendi* arrived at, Davitt and I went back to the meeting and the sessions were resumed. The thunderstorm had cleared the air and a perfect calm reigned during the rest of the proceedings. But the discussions were full and free, as before, and no point was conceded on either side until all arguments for and against had been fully heard. The discussions were conversational and informal, each man keeping his seat as he spoke, and there was not one attempt at a speech. The untoward incident occurred, to the best of my recollection, on the second day of the meeting and it took four days to finish up. I took no notes, but wrote a full report for America while the incidents were fresh in my memory and I have preserved hotel bills and other memoranda which enable me to fix dates and other essential details. Davitt during the whole proceedings kept a pad on his knees, taking voluminous notes, but it was only for the purpose of enabling him to answer arguments, and he destroyed them when the meeting was over. This taking of notes was objected to by one of those opposed to him and was partly responsible for the temporary break.

The final decisions arrived at by the meeting, something of its personnel, a newspaper project which was discussed as a necessity, whether the 'New Departure' was adopted or not, as a means of national propaganda and to destroy the evil influences of Richard Pigott, and other matters incidental to the gathering must be reserved for another chapter.

Chapter 8

The Paris conference ended amicably

I may say at once that no man at that Paris meeting except Davitt was in favour of Parliamentary agitation of any kind, or of interference by Fenians in Parliamentary elections, except in such cases as the Rossa, Kickham and Mitchel elections in Tipperary and Cork. At the time that O'Donovan Rossa was elected for Tipperary he was a treason–felony convict in Chatham Prison, and his election was intended as a rebuke to the Government. Every man who voted for him knew that he would be promptly unseated, and he was. Charles J. Kickham was then put up, with the knowledge that if elected he would refuse to take the Parliamentary oath, even if the election was not declared null and void on the ground that he was ineligible on account of his conviction for treason–felony. John Mitchel was an escaped treason–felony convict and therefore ineligible, but in addition he was liable to be arrested and sent back to prison to serve his unfinished term of penal servitude. He was beaten in Cork, but elected for Tipperary and died Member for that county while the foreign Parliament was engaged in the work of annulling the election. Mitchel would not, under any circumstances, have taken the oath and his election was simply a protest against English rule.

These elections were all demonstrations against the Government and could not be classed as Parliamentary agitation. If similar emergencies should arise again all present would be in favour of taking similar action, but direct participation as an organisation in Parliamentary elections, or support of a Parliamentary Party under any circumstances they were resolutely opposed to. But everyone present had to admit that individual Fenians voted at elections, that some of them openly worked for certain candidates and that Richard Pigott trafficked in Fenian votes by throwing the influence of the *Irishman* in accordance with the bargain he was able to make. In an election in the old Fenian days John Kearney of Millstreet, threw the votes of his friends in favour of the Tory, Major Leader, who was running for Cork, in consideration of £100 paid by the gallant major and which Kearney invested in rifles for use in the rising. Many such instances were cited and it was freely conceded that practically every farmer who was a Fenian voted at all Parliamentary elections.

Then the case of the Longford election, where John Martin[1] was the candidate against Greville, a chip of a Guardsman, whom the priests supported by the most extraordinary misuse of their power and influence over the people, was a most remarkable instance of departure from the regular Fenian policy. John Martin, although a fellow-prisoner of Mitchel and his brother-in-law, was in favour of Parliamentary action and was nominated in the regular way with the knowledge that if elected he would enter Parliament and take the oath. Yet every Fenian in Ireland was in favour of his election and thousands of them poured into Longford to help his supporters resist the wholesale intimidation organised by Father Reynolds of St Mel's College, with the silent consent, if not the open approval, of Bishop Woodlock.[2] They joined hands with A. M. Sullivan of the *Nation*,[3] their arch enemy, and at the head of crowds of sturdy men brought in by the local leaders from Cavan, Westmeath, Meath, Kildare and King's County, well-known Fenians put an end to intimidation by hard fighting. The Longford Fenians all voted and worked for Martin and no protest was made from any quarter against this open support of a Parliamentary candidate who intended to take the oath of allegiance and later took it.

All these things were brought out in the discussion and it was made clear that Fenianism had often been, and would probably often be again, a decisive factor in Parliamentary elections. But all that was said in favour of defining the conditions under which this interference should take place, or that votes always cast could be used intelligently to influence public policy, was of no avail. As an organisation they would not engage in Parliamentary politics, but no restrictions were placed on individual voting. On the question of Fenians going into Parliament and taking the oath there was no disagreement whatever. All were opposed to it.

The same attitude was adopted towards the Land Question. Kickham had very strong sympathy with the farmers and labourers and welcomed every concession that tended in the smallest degree to improve their condition, but he was just as strongly opposed to direct Fenian partici-pation in agrarian agitation as he was to interference in Parliamentary work. He thought the farmers would get on better without Fenian help and that the indirect effects of Fenianism would be of more real value to the farmers, as instanced by the Gladstone Land Act of 1870, than would any aid that could be given through public agitation.

Besides Davitt there was only one man present who differed materially with Kickham on this point, and that was Matthew Harris,[4] of Ballinasloe, who was afterwards a Member of Parliament. He was strongly of the opinion that an agrarian agitation could be made a powerful revolutionary weapon, but at that time, so far as I could judge from his talk, he seemed to think that the agitation should be entirely outside Parliament and free from the control of any Parliamentary Party. The rest were decidedly opposed to Fenian interference in agrarian or Parliamentary agitation. At the time the meeting was held – January 1879 – the coming agricultural crisis was foreseen by close observers, but not by those who had no special knowledge, and even Davitt was without the stimulus with which conditions in the West of Ireland supplied him a few months later.

But the necessity of a public National Movement that would help Ireland's claim before the world, foster a sound and healthy public opinion in the country and secure control of the municipal and other local public bodies, so far as the restricted franchise that then existed would permit, was recognised by all. In the course of the discussion on this phase of the subject, some who favoured the principle of capturing the local bodies were not sanguine of a large measure of success, first on account of the limited number of Fenians who were rate-payers, and secondly, because of the difficulty of securing enough of reliable men to fill the places. Cases were cited where there were two or three bright, intelligent young men in a family, but the father only had a vote. There was also the objection that the proposed interference in public affairs would bring the members more directly under the notice of the government and make the work of the police easier. But this objection told with infinitely greater force against such demonstrations as the Rossa, Kickham and Mitchel elections, and to some extent the Longford elections, although in the latter case Fenians and Moderates joined hands.

After a full discussion lasting two days, all agreed that a public organisation was necessary and that so far as possible Nationalists should be elected as Town Councillors, Town Commissioners and Poor Law Guardians, and the work of formulating a plan of operations was left to a committee which remained behind after the full meeting had adjourned.

On one point there was perfect unanimity throughout the meeting – that Richard Pigott's power for mischief must be destroyed, either by depriving him of the control of the *Irishman* or by starting a weekly paper in Dublin that would be recognised as a national organ and would deprive him of his Fenian readers. Even among those men who disliked and distrusted Pigott it was demonstrated to me that his power for mischief was very great. The *Irishman* had persistently misrepresented Davitt's American speeches and most of those present had seen no other reports of them. But my letter, which was the subject of much discussion at the meeting, had appeared in the *Freeman* and I naturally thought that those who discussed it had all read the full text in that paper. I found, however, that only two or three had read it and that the rest had only read a summary of it in the *Irishman*. Among these was Kickham.

The summary was done by Pigott himself and was a masterpiece of skilful misrepresentation. Long extracts were correctly given, but between them were running comments and descriptions of the omitted parts, artfully suggesting that the intention was the betrayal of the Fenian cause and a retreat from the objective of national independence covered by a breastwork of false pretences. For some time it was the *Irishman's* hostile reports of Davitt's speeches and Pigott's dishonest version of my letter that were discussed and this had much to do with the early friction. When the Fenian leaders were thus misled how much worse was the plight of the rank and file who knew nothing of Pigott's dishonesty?

Pigott was financially, as well as politically, dishonest, because he lived a life of debauchery that required money beyond his resources. His father, a rugged, fine old man, whom I remember well, had been bookkeeper in the old *Nation*, and when Denis Holland started the *Irishman* it seemed the natural thing to make his son the business manager. On Holland's failure, P. J. Smyth took hold of it for a time and his articles, and those contributed by John Edward Pigot, the weak-kneed but sincere Nationalist son of the Chief Baron of that name, and no relative of Richard, gave the paper a good literary and political standing. Richard Pigott got hold of it from Smyth, and the *Irish People* having been suppressed, he commenced at once to cater for Fenian support. By securing Dr Sigerson,[5] as chief editorial writer, and later James O'Connor,[6] an ex-Fenian prisoner, as sub-editor, he established the reputation of the paper as a sound Nationalist organ.

The life of Richard Pigott when written will make an interesting, but very dark chapter in Irish history, and the dark spots do not begin with the Parnell Commission. From the first he was dishonest. He allowed Dr Sigerson to write fine articles and James O'Connor to print the news of interest to Nationalists, but he skilfully manipulated the policy of the paper so as to enable him to sell its influence when the opportunity offered. Opportunities never failed and Parliamentary elections offered him a rich harvest.

The *Irishman* became the medium for the collection of all kinds of funds and Pigott stole impartially from all of them – prisoners' defence funds, testimonials and 'tributes' alike – and he did not hesitate to seize a portion of a large sum sent from New York to the Fenians at home by the released political prisoners in 1871, the draft having been unfortunately made payable to him.

The scandal caused by this theft was the cause of the attempt to murder David Murphy, a former Fenian 'centre' of Limerick, who was Pigott's bookkeeper. Murphy threatened to expose his dishonesty and Pigott promptly made a false accusation that Murphy was a spy and had him shot, but fortunately the wound was not mortal.

At the time of the Paris meeting Pigott, while posing as an extreme and irreconcilable Nationalist and denouncing Davitt and Devoy as backsliders, had really mortgaged himself to the Parliamentarians of the day. Isaac Butt had more than once raised money for Pigott, and on the last occasion had obtained large sums from Mr William Shaw,[7] Mitchell-Henry,[8] Sir Joseph Neale McKenna[9] and others. I was informed at the meeting that the amount was £3,000 that Butt had taken a mortgage on the *Irishman* for the amount, as security and to enable him to keep a 'Sword of Damocles' suspended over Pigott's head. I was further informed that Mr Butt had given power of attorney to Patrick Egan to act for him.

This financial situation was the lever with which it was hoped to oust Pigott from control of the *Irishman*. If he refused to get out then it was proposed to start a genuine Nationalist paper that would drive him out of business. Davitt undertook to ask Patrick Egan to foreclose Butt's mortgage and was very confident that he would succeed. Davitt's report on this matter was made at a meeting held some months later in Dublin and will be dealt with at the proper time.

The meeting began to count its chickens before they were hatched and devoted some time to selecting an editor for the paper that had not yet been born or bought. Davitt renewed his proposition that I should remain in Paris and direct the paper and was supported by many. I declined the offer and explained that no man living in Paris could edit a paper in Dublin. As I could not live in Dublin until my fifteen years' sentence should expire, I was therefore eliminated.

Davitt strongly favoured O'Kelly, but one or two present had objections and he was dropped. A Cork man proposed William O'Brien,[10] Matt Harris strongly seconded him and several spoke in his favour, but nobody could tell whether he would accept or not. Most of them called him 'Willie' O'Brien, not William, and all spoke very highly of him. The final choice of an editor was put off until a future meeting when progress could be reported on the business end of the proposition. I may say here that there was no difficulty about funds; there was ample money at the disposal of that meeting.

There were many views as to the character and form of the paper. Some concerned themselves wholly with its literary standard and political tone, others talked of its presentation of news, but Matt Harris struck me as having the most original view. 'My idea of a paper that will catch the masses,' he said, 'is one with a big splatther of a cartoon on the front page. A man will be going home from work, he'll see it displayed in a shop window and stop and look at it. Then if he likes the cartoon and has the tuppence he'll say, "Be gob, I'll buy that paper".'

There was a general laugh, but there was a great deal in the idea. Matt was disgusted with the fare in the hotel. He had a healthy appetite and ordered two plates of every dish served. 'I don't wonder that the Prussians knocked the devil out of these Frenchmen,' he said. 'They don't eat half enough.'

Their *petits verres*[11] also disgusted him. A few of us, after having eaten the stingy dinner at the little hotel, went into the Café de Cluny to get a cup of black coffee. Harris didn't care for coffee and said he'd take a glass of brandy. The waiter brought his decanter with the measure marked by lines and filled a *petit verre*. 'And is that the thing they offer *a man* for a glass of brandy?' he asked. 'Take it away and bring me a decent glass.' The situation was explained to the waiter and he brought a larger glass and the sturdy Galway man tossed off 'three fingers' without bothering with a 'chaser'. Professor Sullivan, of the Cork Queen's College, had been there recently and had also preferred the goblet to the 'pony', and most Irishmen visiting Paris do the same thing.

That ended the Paris meeting. The committee met after the adjournment.

Chapter 9

Parnell's relations with Clan na Gael

The committee appointed to draw up the programme remained in Paris for several days after the meeting adjourned, discussed the situation thoroughly, but did not succeed in formulating any definite plan. The principal thing it did was to remove the obstacles that stood in the way of Fenians taking part in a public movement of a really national character and co-operating with Nationalists who were not Fenians. The rest was put off for a future meeting.

Kickham became ill and was anxious to get home. He could not travel alone, so on 3 February three of us started with him for Dieppe. The four were a majority of a Directory of seven men who formed the supreme governing body of the Irish Revolutionary movement throughout the world – three representing Ireland and Great Britain, three the United States and Canada and one Australia and New Zealand. This body had been established in 1876 and had already opened communication with two of the governments of Europe. If we four could agree on a plan for a public movement it would have the undivided support of a compactly organised and thoroughly disciplined body of 50,000 men, on three continents, whose average of intelligence was very high. We already had the support of the American division: the governing body of the home organisation had given their representatives freedom of action within certain limits, and Australasia would endorse anything agreed on by Ireland and America. The discussion was continued on the journey, as we were in a compartment by ourselves on the train.

Kickham got sick on the train. He had a very bad stomach and a railroad journey had the same effect on him as the rolling of a ship. He suffered great pain, and when Kickham's stomach was bad the world was coming to an end. We had to get off at Amiens, put up at a hotel and remain over night. One of the party had a hobby for cathedrals[1] and we took Kickham to see the cathedral at Amiens.

There was a first communion procession going on and a small army of boys and girls tastefully dressed in white marched into the church as we entered. Kickham was intensely religious and the sight brought tears of joy to his eyes – for he could see just enough to realise what it was. He had seen a doctor the evening before and had got some medicine which had done him good, but the first communion procession cured him completely and put him in good humour. Leaning over to me while the beautifully dressed children were marching by singing, and alluding to our escort, he said jokingly: 'As long as he has this hobby about cathedrals there is some hope for him. The grace of God'll strike him some time or other.'[2]

We resumed our journey, but another hour on the train made Kickham sick again, but our friend insisted on his holding on till we reached Rouen, where there were two cathedrals, one of which, that of St Ouen, had an Irish rector named McCartan. After a rest we took Kickham to see the cathedrals. When we reached St Ouen's, the moon was shining from behind one side of the church, giving a beautiful effect of light and shade. The lower part of the building was dark, but the light gray of the little minarets and turrets was turned into a silvery hue. Kickham stood gazing up, lost in admiration, and at last said: 'What wonderful faith the men who built those cathedrals must have had.'

He was loath to leave the spot and our two friends started for the hotel, leaving Kickham and me standing there. When we turned to go our friends were out of sight and we were in a most peculiar fix. We had been guided there by one of the party who knew Rouen well, but I had never been there before and I did not know either the name of the hotel or the street on which it was situated. We had gone there from the railroad station in a bus and through different streets than those which led to the church. I at first concealed my embarrassment from Kickham, but he guessed it and peppered me with questions, growing more excited every minute.

As his questions were put to me by word of mouth and I had to answer on the fingers of his left hand, which had an old woollen glove on it, a crowd of boys gathered, took it for granted that I was a dummy and followed us jeering, 'Anglish maun: oh, damn.' At last I had to convince the gamins that I was neither a dummy nor an Englishman by a few plain words of Algerian French that sent them scampering off.

After much tramping, by sheer luck we came to a street near the railway station which I knew we had passed through before, and then I speedily found the way to the hotel – which bore the same resemblance to the other hotels as one pea does to another. When we were safe inside and found our two friends quietly smoking over the coffee 'the gentle Charles' again exploded and gave them 'a piece of his mind' over their base desertion, insisting that it was only my marvellous topographical instinct which had saved him from a night in the streets.

We went next day to Dieppe, finished our consultation there and put Kickham on the boat for New Haven, whence his guide (the Secretary) saw him safely to Dublin, where he then lived. I had reason to believe that a 'shadow' had picked us up at Dieppe, so, partly to break the pursuit and partly to see the town which Owen Roe O'Neill had so brilliantly defended, my other friend and I returned by way of Beauvais and Arras, making the journey from Beauvais to Arras on foot. I also walked out from Arras to see the battlefield of Bapaume, where my old commander in Algeria, General Faidherbe,[3] whose signature is on my discharge, had checked the Prussian advance on Havre and relieved for a brief spell the gloom which overspread France by one brilliant victory.

I got back to Paris on 11 February, and found a letter from Davitt awaiting me. He had seen a number of men and felt very hopeful that the projected new public movement only needed explanation to make it take with the rank and file of the Fenians, and that the outside Nationalists would have no hesitation in joining it if properly launched. He had seen Parnell, and Parnell had expressed a wish to see me and talk the matter over.

One of the things arranged at the meeting in Paris was that I should make a tour of the organisation in Ireland and Great Britain, see things for myself, ascertain the views of the men from their own lips and be able to report what I had found when I returned to America. I was not asked to go, on account of the risk, but on hearing my determination to take the chances, it was agreed that a series of meetings should be arranged for me.

The Fenian prisoners released in 1871 had received a 'conditional pardon' which exiled them from 'the United Kingdom' for the balance of their respective sentences, and my sentence of fifteen years' penal servitude would expire on 19 February 1882. If caught I was therefore liable to be put back in a convict prison until that date.

In order to have a free talk with Parnell it would be better to have it in France, so as to make it less risky for him. I was later agreeably surprised to find that Parnell had no hesitation whatever in taking such risks. There was another risk for me in meeting Parnell which I regarded as worse than being arrested – that is of misrepresentation of what had occurred between us – and I foresaw it as clearly then as I have been made to feel it ever since.

Davitt had made a series of engagements which prevented him from coming, and he deemed it best that he should not. I therefore wrote him, stipulating that another gentleman whose word would be taken by every Fenian worth his salt – one of those who had been present at the Paris meeting and who was on the committee to draw up the platform – should be present with me at the interview. I am not at liberty to name him,[4] because he still lives under the authority of British law, and I am sorry it is so, for his testimony would be of infinite value. He had had an interview with Parnell about a year before, in company with others, and I am fortunately able to give a report of that interview by one of the participants.

Finding that I insisted on having another man present, Parnell decided to adopt a similar course and notified me, through Davitt, that he would be accompanied by Joseph G. Biggar. The place selected was Boulogne and the date set was 7 March 1879.

As Parnell's first word on my friend introducing me referred to the previous meeting, and as that meeting really began our connection with Parnell, it is proper that I should give here a report of it received within the last few days from the gentleman who represented the Clan na Gael at the gathering. The following extracts from a letter from Dr William Carroll will speak for themselves:

617 South Sixteenth Street
Philadelphia, 24 July 1906

Dear Devoy: . . .

Our definite understanding to set in at least a friendly way towards Parnell may, I think, be dated from the day, early in 1878, when the released Fenians, Sergeant McCarthy,[5] Corporal Chambers,[6] and, I think Davitt, arrived in Dublin after their release. Parnell was giving them breakfast at his (Morrison's) hotel when somebody told him I was at the Hibernian Hotel in Dawson Street. Immediately he gave a friend an invitation for me to join them at breakfast, but was told by the friend that I wished to pass unnoticed.

After the breakfast, at which you may remember, Sergeant McCarthy died on the stairway, Mr Parnell came to my room in the Hibernian Hotel and alone we went over the political situation. I asked him if he was in favour of the absolute independence of Ireland. He replied that he was and that as soon as the people so declared he would go with them. I then told him that we would be his friends and would ask our friends there to support him in all he did towards that end. I met him several times afterwards in London, always on the most friendly terms and with the same understanding.

At that time their party in Parliament consisted of himself, Biggar, O'Sullivan of Kilmallock,[7] O'Donnell[8] and O'Connor Power, and without the support of the original Butt Home Rulers, which they had practically, although not entirely lost, the support of the Fenian element was of vital importance to them, but was not to be easily had, as the Supreme Council had recently placed them under a ban – which I do not know that they ever entirely removed – although at a meeting we had near Manchester, England, at which Davitt, Chambers and other Fenians met the Parliamentarians and I.R.B. men, a *modus vivendi* was agreed upon which enabled both to go on with their work without clashing.

At a meeting held in my room in a little private hotel off the Strand in London, at which Parnell, O'Sullivan, of Kilmallock; ——, —— and —— were present, while all were absolutely in accord as to absolute separation as the end, there was a fierce and loud dispute between —— and —— as to the extent of support to be given the public by the secret movement in bringing about the desired end, a dispute which was abruptly closed by the occupant of the next room giving a significant cough and then shuffling his feet across the room to let us know that he had heard, and did not want to hear, what was going on in my room.

The next morning I found that he was a prominent officer of Her Majesty's Government in Ireland, at whose elbow I had sat at a Trinity College banquet in Dublin a short time before, and whose Irish feelings, Conservative though he was, made him notify us that he did not want us to get into trouble through the exercise of his official duties.

During my sojourn in London and Dublin I frequently met all the prominent supporters of the public movement and did all I could to smooth over their difficulties with the I.R.B. extreme men, and, as you well know, the Clan men received Parnell, Dillon and Davitt with open arms, giving the latter $310 as the proceeds of his first lecture in Philadelphia – the first money he received on this side of the Atlantic, and managing Parnell and Dillon's tour.

In all of which I think we did right in the light of the then under-standing of their attitude towards the Fenians. But when on the day of Parnell's departure from New York he announced his previously formu-lated Land League, the officers of which were, in several instances hostile to the Clan, and the whole movement threatened to submerge the I.R.B., I, as you know, then and there severed all connection with Parliamentary agitation, although I never tried to start any war on them or their ways, leaving time and the results to settle all that.

Ever sincerely yours,
William Carroll

The men present at that London meeting whose names are omitted in the above letter are still living under British jurisdiction. One is a Member of Parliament, another was the Secretary of the Fenian organisation at home,[9] and the other was the gentleman who accompanied me to meet Parnell in Boulogne.[10] As Dr Carroll was then the chief officer of the Clan na Gael and was its envoy in Ireland, the significance of the meeting will be easily understood. It had nothing of a social character and was concerned only with Irish National politics. The gentleman who coughed and shuffled his feet as a friendly warning did not keep entirely silent on the subject, for I read some time ago in the Recollections of a Scotland Yard Detective in *Reynolds's Newspaper* a version of the story. The gentleman was Mr Gibson, then one of the Members of Parliament for Trinity College and, if I am not mistaken, Solicitor-General for Ireland, and afterwards Lord Ashbourne.[11]

Among the released prisoners present with Mr Parnell when Sergeant McCarthy fell dead was also John Patrick O'Brien,[12] now a resident of Dublin. It was on the invitation of Professor Galbraith[13] that Dr Carroll attended the Trinity College dinner at which he met the future Lord Ashbourne.

Readers of *The Gaelic American* in this country need no information as to the character and standing of Dr Carroll, but the younger generation in Ireland may require a little light. Dr Carroll was a Sergeant-Major in the Union Army, served all through the American Civil War and for some time after it, in care of the wounded. No man stands higher among all classes of citizens in Philadelphia than Dr Carroll. He is a Donegal Presbyterian and was an intimate friend of John Mitchel. When Mitchel was returning to Ireland in 1874, Dr Carroll came to New York to see him off. Standing on the deck Mitchel said to him, half in jest, 'I wish you were coming with me, doctor.' Dr Carroll, in spite of Mitchel's protest that he was not serious, immediately went out, sent a telegram to a medical friend in Philadelphia to look after his patients, bought a few shirts, collars and cuffs in the nearest dry goods store, and a ticket at the dock office and started with Mitchel for Ireland, where he took care of him during his first trip. That act gives the character of the man.

With Dr Carroll's account of his interviews with Parnell and his reference to the cause of the sudden break-up of the London Conference, the reader will more readily grasp the significance of the Boulogne meeting and two subsequent meetings which I had with Parnell in Dublin.

Chapter 10

With Parnell and Biggar in Boulogne

——————

On coming back from Arras I moved from the Hotel Des Missions Étrangères to the Hotel de Seine in the Rue de Seine, which was largely patronised by Spanish-Americans and other foreign students.[1] The change was made necessary by the appearance of our having been shadowed, but I arranged to have my meetings with others take place elsewhere. Davitt came once to Paris after his return from the meeting, but that was only for a day or two before my departure for England.[2] We did our talking sitting at a table in a café or walking along the street.

My friend, who was to be my colleague in the conference with Parnell, and I started for Boulogne, in accordance with the arrangement made with Davitt, and we arrived the night before the time set. I had been there for a fortnight eighteen years before on my way to Algeria, and found in one of the hotels an Irish head waiter named O'Connor, the son of a refugee of 1848, and an Irish interpreter named Neville, who had served in the Foreign Legion and was the son of an officer of the British army, who had been ruined by horse-racing. Neville spoke French much better than English. The ex-head waiter was still alive in 1879, and had been promoted, but the soldier had died. It was in this hotel, which had changed its name from the Hotel de l'Europe to the Hotel du Louvre, that Parnell, Biggar, my unnamed friend and I stopped during the conference.

We met Parnell and Biggar as they stepped off the gang plank of the Folkestone steamer, while the fishwomen in their sabots were clattering down to carry off the passengers' baggage, an occupation for women which shocked Parnell and greatly amused Biggar. We stood a few yards away and Parnell, at once recognising my friend, made toward us. I was introduced to Parnell and he then introduced both of us to Biggar. There was a little park which reached to the water front, and on a bench in this park we took our seats and commenced our talk. The first words of greeting were exchanged as we walked to the seat, and my friend at once asked Mr Parnell how his mother and sisters were, and Parnell answered with great particularity, showing how good the personal relations were between them. As a matter of fact, the relations of the Parnell family with Fenianism might be said to have begun when Mrs Parnell,[3] leading one of her sons, who was not Charles, by the hand, walked into the office of the *Irish People* in Dublin and paid a subscription for the paper. Fanny Parnell,[4] at a very early age, also wrote poetry in the *Irish People* under the *nom de plume* of 'Aleria'.

As we took our seats on the bench, Parnell, with a twinkle in his eye, said: 'The last time I had the pleasure of meeting Mr —— he started a hare in the person of John O'Connor Power, and we were so busy chasing that hare during the whole evening that we had no time for anything else. Now, I hope Mr —— won't start a hare this time.'

Mr —— smiled good humouredly at this allusion to the interrupted interview in London, which Dr Carroll's letter describes. The remark showed plainly Parnell's regret that an understanding had not been arrived at by those present at that meeting which was highly representative of all the then active elements of Irish National politics at both sides of the Atlantic.

We chatted for a considerable time on the bench in the little park, nobody else being within hearing, and then went into the Hotel du Louvre for dinner, which we took in a small room that we had entirely to ourselves, and there we remained for the rest of the evening discussing the Irish political situation. The talk was at first very general and at all times informal.

Biggar did a great deal of the talking. He had been for a short time a Fenian, and was a member of the governing body in Ireland, but had been removed from it by the making of a rule which debarred Members of Parliament. He was given the choice of giving up one or the other and had decided to stay in Parliament. He did not seem to feel aggrieved at this action, but was very free in expressing his contempt for everything in Parliament – its membership, its rules and its forms of procedure. It afforded many ways of helping Ireland, if Ireland would only send the right kind of men there, but he was very free in admitting that the chief good that could be done was in the way of blocking English business. Anyhow he was there and he did not propose to get out. Resigning from anything was a mistake. He had once resigned from the Water Board in Belfast, in disgust at the way things were carried on, but when they were rid of him matters became much worse, and he had been sorry ever since that he had not stayed.

Biggar did not seem to judge things from any settled principle or conviction, but from some side light or detail which impressed him. His own expulsion from the Fenian organisation arose through the fight with O'Connor Power, which had raised the question of a man's taking two contradictory oaths, but the latter did not bother Biggar at all. If the man's action pleased him he did not seem to care how many oaths he took.

After hearing something of a homily on the dishonour involved in the taking of the Parliamentary oath by a Fenian, he had remarked dryly that he had never cared for O'Connor Power since he had seen him pay three and sixpence for his dinner in the House of Commons. This extravagance he seemed to regard as due to the demoralising effect of aristocratic surroundings, but he did not say so; he simply recorded the fact.

I said to him: 'Mr Biggar, I am sorry you turned Catholic. You were a great deal more use to us as a Presbyterian. Now your conversion will be pointed to as a warning to young Protestants of Nationalist leanings to keep away from us, lest the Pope should get hold of them.'

Biggar laughed in a dry way at this, but did not agree with it, but Parnell did. Biggar then went into a long explanation of how the doctrine of Predestination had repelled him, even in early youth, and how he had gradually become a Freethinker. But after some years he had arrived at the conclusion that *some* religion must be right and it became a question whether he would adopt one that was all dogmatic or one which allowed him to use his private judgment within certain limits. He finally came to the conclusion that no man or church had a right to define those limits, and that he must either exercise his private judgment fully or wholly surrender it. Therefore – evidently without being fully convinced – he had become a Catholic.

Biggar's physical appearance was as odd as his mental make-up. A low-sized squat man, with a powerful body, his arms were much longer than the average, one shoulder wider than the other, the face unprepossessing, the large head set unevenly between the shoulders and seeming to have corners on it, he looked anything but a political leader. His clothes were as odd as his bodily form, and looked as if they had been 'thrown on with a pitchfork'. His coat was a sort of brownish-black, and was of very ample proportions, his vest was of some indescribable yellowish tint and long enough for a six-footer, while a wisp of a blue cotton tie with white spots on it, knotted loosely under the collar, hung down over his shirt front. I don't remember anything particular about the trousers, so they must have been normal. On the whole, he looked like a country huxter of a previous generation. But, with all his oddities of mind and body and speech, Biggar was a man of unusual force of character, and there could be no mistaking his sincerity. His hatred of England was intense, but he expressed it in a quiet, matter-of-fact way, without any appearance of heat or feeling.

Biggar's theological disquisitions took up so much time and diverted our minds so much from the subject we had met to discuss that I was sorry for making my remark at that particular time, though the explanation interested me very much. We got back to earth again, and Parnell tried to convince us that we attached too little importance to the work that could be done in Parliament if the right men were there to do it. He freely admitted that Parliamentary work should only play a secondary part, and must be in conjunction with a movement in Ireland. But there was no such movement then, and he was sure that an important part of the work of creating one could be done effectively in the British House of Commons. He had great hope in the young men, and expressed the belief that if the men who thought as we did in Ireland would use steadily the same energy they had thrown into the Mitchel election in Tipperary great results would be achieved.

Parnell's talk was very quiet, but very plain and direct. There was neither equivocation nor reserve about it. He knew he was talking to men who represented the whole Irish revolutionary movement at home and abroad, and he wanted to convince them that they would serve the ultimate ends of that movement by helping him. He was not trying to convert them, or asking them to give up their policy of seeking complete Separation from England, or their belief that it could only be finally won by physical force. His object was to convince them that Constitutional and Parliamentary agitation, conducted in the way he would conduct it if he had the power, would not injure their movement, but would give them control of many agencies of advancing their cause that were not then within their reach.

He did not say definitely, and we did not ask him to say, whether he would prefer Total Separation, Repeal of the Union, or some form of Legislative Independence involving some connection with England, but the impression he left on me was very distinct that he had not his mind made up as to which was the best, or the one most likely to be realised, but that he would go with the Irish people to the fullest limit in breaking up the existing form of connection with England. In other words, he was an opportunist, prepared to go to the utmost length that circumstances seemed to justify to obtain by any available means the largest possible degree of National Independence for Ireland.

I don't profess to be an infallible judge of men, but I have met a great many public men, both Irish and American – and I met Parnell several times after that – and can safely say that not one of them ever went more directly to his subject, or left less room for misunderstanding his mean-ing than Parnell. There has been much nonsense written and spoken about Parnell's 'mystery' and 'reticence', while extracting unconditional promises from loquacious men. Parnell was reticent in the best sense, but he was also frank at that meeting in Boulogne.

An instance of his frankness and of his readiness to throw off the reserve that was natural to him occurred in the course of the first even-ing's talk in the private room of the hotel. In explaining his ideas of parliamentary politics he mentioned a recent election in the County Down, where he had advised the Nationalists to support Lord Castlereagh (afterwards Marquis of Londonderry),[5] who was the Tory candidate, instead of Sharman Crawford,[6] who, if I remember rightly, was the Liberal candidate, as a matter of tactics. I told him I believed it was a mistake to advise any Irishman to vote for a man with the infamous name or title of Castlereagh, and that the family of the wretch should be kept forever out of public life in Ireland.

Parnell immediately warmed up, his eyes flashed and his whole manner showed unmistakable irritation. He said such doctrine was nonsense and that by beating a Whig by voting for a Tory, or a Tory by voting for a Whig, when we could not elect our own man, was good politics and that this was the case in Down. The point was that 'any stick was good enough to beat the dog with', and I admitted it as a general proposition, but contended that it should not hold good in the case of notorious traitors, else the national moral sense would be impaired. Parnell was not an idealist, and his mind did not run in the same groove as that of Gaelic Irishmen, but addressed itself coolly to the material proposition that confronted him for the moment. He felt so strongly at fault being found with him over this Castlereagh matter that he recurred to it more than once during the evening.

The second day of our sojourn in Boulogne was a Sunday. The party breakfasted together in the same private room, and we sat there chatting for a considerable time. Parnell was very much interested in my Foreign Legion experiences and my having starved in Boulogne on my way to enlist. When I told him of Napoleon's old camp on the hill, where he had assembled a large army for an invasion of England that never came off he expressed a desire to see it and we walked out to it. He took the deepest interest in the whole subject, looked carefully at the monument, and as we strolled over the ground speculated on what conditions might exist had that finest army in Europe, led by the greatest general of all time, succeeded in landing in England.

We extended our walk a good deal and at last saw groups of sturdy little French infantrymen industriously plucking something in the fields and making it into nice little bunches as they went along. Parnell asked were they picking flowers, but I told him they were gathering radishes to eat with the portion of meat they got in their soup. The were little red roots like radishes, but Parnell was not satisfied and, as a group of soldiers came up, each with a bunch in his hand he insisted on me asking one of the men. The soldier told me they were not radishes, but another root which resembled the radish, and the name of which I forget, but they were for the purpose of flavouring their dinner, as I had said.

Parnell looked at them silently for a moment and then said: 'I don't wonder these fellows were able to tramp all over Europe and make themselves comfortable where other men would starve.'

We were standing on elevated ground and Parnell's eye had been turned repeatedly to some fishing craft anchored close to the shore outside the little harbour. Before the soldiers left he told me to ask them where those vessels got their fish, and the information came promptly that they caught mackerel off the coast of Ireland. 'Ah! I thought so,' said Parnell. 'These are the fellows that catch our mackerel by permission of the English Government. We'll stop that some time.'

Parnell's mind was on the details of the Irish Question all the time, rather than on any general plan of settlement, and it is probable that he never had any such plan in his head at all. That remark about the mackerel and the other about the French soldiers were only two of many made during those two days in Boulogne which indicated the way his mind was working.

Boulogne-sur-Mer was once a fortified town, and the old wall and fortifications were in 1879 crowded every Sunday with sightseers. We 'took them in' on our way back from Napoleon's camp. Chatting as we slowly walked along, we stopped at several points until we came to an old bastion where we divided into two groups and remained a considerable time. The fact that most of this day's talk, wholly informal as it was, took place amid military surroundings, gave the conversation a decided military turn. Parnell and I were in one corner, Biggar and my colleague in the other.

Parnell freely admitted that he had no objection on principle to insurrection, but objected to attempts to fight England without first creating the conditions which would give Ireland a fair chance. He pointed out how England had been able to force a crisis in all recent insurrectionary movements by a policy of repression that got the fighting blood of the Irish up and made them strike at a time when there was no decent chance of even making a good fight. He was surprised to find that I agreed with all this, and told him that every Nationalist in America whose judgment was worth considering was of the same opinion.

Roughly speaking, I found that Parnell was in full agreement with the policy which the leaders of the Clan na Gael had publicly avowed in their declarations published a short time previously: 'Peace at home for the present, but vigorous attacks on England abroad, wherever and whenever possible.' He inquired minutely as to the number of trained men available for small expeditions that could be sent, for instance, to help the Boers, or the Indians, or the Mahdi, and was gratified when I told him that the number, mostly men who had served in the American Regular army, was far greater than the means of arming or transporting them. He was filled with the idea that a strong and vigorous agitation at home would keep the eyes of the American Irish fixed on Ireland, stimulate their interest, and enable us to gather up the resources, then lacking, which would be necessary to carry out such a policy. His approval of that policy was outspoken and unreserved, and he promised that if we entered on it with vigour he would give a good account of himself in fighting the estimates in the House of Commons. Even if we failed to come to an agreement Parnell was satisfied that the adoption of such a policy by us would have practically the same effect as a treaty of alliance.

On our way back to the hotel we told Biggar of the line our conversation had taken, and he chuckled with delight over the fun they would be able to raise in the House of Commons when things began to get lively for England abroad, but was disappointed to learn that our financial resources would not enable us to begin at once and on a large scale. My colleague, however, was not enamoured with these schemes, which he regarded as somewhat wild, and was more intent on the political education of the Irish people by a literary propaganda. However, as these matters were only discussed informally in conversation, no decision binding anyone was arrived at. But the discussion had very much to do with clearing the way for the working agreement by which the Clan na Gael in America afterwards gave its support to Parnell and provided him with the 'sinews of war'.

We returned to the hotel, and in a more formal discussion found that we could not agree on a definite plan of united action, but that many of the obstacles had been removed. We at least understood each other better. But, while we were unable to make an agreement binding the two bodies, and there were some points of difference between Parnell and my colleague which seemed unlikely to be removed, I found that Parnell was prepared to go more than half way to meet us. It seems necessary to say again that even at that time (in the early days of March, 1879) there was no question of starting a purely agrarian movement. What we were thinking of was a distinctly National public movement. Events in Ireland, which were the result of the terribly wet season, changed all that in a few weeks, but Parnell and Biggar were as ignorant of what was in store for the country when they left Boulogne as was the rest of the world.

Chapter 11

Sought alliances with foreign powers

_____

Letters from America and Ireland were awaiting me on my return to Paris, and in a few days the Secretary came with the information regarding the arrangements he had made for a series of meetings I was to attend, first in England and Scotland, and then in Ireland. As these were all for the transaction of purely Fenian business, I shall only deal with such portions of their proceedings as had any connection with Davitt or concerned the public movement.

My American letters dealt in part with an effort made by a few men in New York to offset the 'New Departure' by bringing James Stephens to America with a view to making him the leader of the revolutionary movement at home and abroad with dictatorial powers. As the old man was then visibly failing in intellect, the attempt had not a ghost of a chance of success, but it was bought to a sudden and inglorious end at a meeting in New York by the vigorous stand of the Clan na Gael men, led by Dr Carroll and John J. Breslin. The incident would make an interesting, but painful chapter for which I have ample material, but it would be out of place here.

One of Dr Carroll's letters directed me to call at the American consulate for a letter sent in care of Consul-General Hooper and I called and found the following from Senator Conover, of Florida:[1]

UNITED STATES SENATE CHAMBER,
WASHINGTON, 3 March 1879.
Hon. E. W. Stoughton, Minister, etc., St Petersburg,[2] and others whom it may concern:

The bearer of this letter, Mr John Devoy, whom I know personally well, is abroad as the representative of the 'Irish National Directory' and authorised to present their case to Continental Governments.

I bespeak for him that courtesy which is due him, not only in his representative capacity, but as a gentleman of the highest order of ability and integrity, and entitled to full confidence everywhere.

Respectfully,
S. B. Conover

Senator Conover was the grandson of an Ulster Presbyterian United Irishman who had to fly to America in 1798. He had served in the Union Army as a surgeon and Dr Carroll and he became intimate friends during the Civil War. After the war he settled in Florida and was elected United States Senator by a Legislature in which there was no Irish vote but his own. He joined the Clan na Gael after his election and never was under any obligation to it, but was able to render it many important services. During the *Catalpa* expedition he arranged with us that the vessel was to land the rescued prisoners at Fernandina, Florida, where the Collector of the Port, a protégé of his, would receive them on the United States revenue cutter and then send them North, while the barque continued her whaling voyage to make more money to clear the expenses and provide funds for future operations. This plan was spoiled by the impatience of the rescued men to get to their journey's end, which induced Breslin to change the plan agreed on and make for New York.

In 1877, Senator Conover introduced a Clan na Gael delegation to the representative of a certain European power in Washington, and by arrangement with the Minister, was made the medium of future communications. The references made by that Minister in his talk with us to the presentation of loyal addresses to scions of the English royal family visiting Ireland, and to the very limited demands of the Irish Members of Parliament, which created the belief abroad that there was no real National movement in Ireland, had very much to do with winning over the leaders of the Clan na Gael to the 'New Departure'. As the Minister spoke English very poorly, most of the interview was conducted in French, and I was the interpreter. That part of his talk certainly made a deep impression on me, and I referred to it pointedly in the speech I made at Davitt's Brooklyn lecture in 1878.

In 1877 one of the men who was afterwards present at the London meeting with Parnell, described in Dr Carroll's letter, and whose name I withhold because he is still under the thumb of the British Government, was in Madrid and had interviews with Castelar,[3] Figueras[4] and Pi y Margall,[5] with a view to co-operation with the Irish for the capture of Gibraltar. When Dr Carroll was in Europe in 1878, the Republic having been overthrown, the same man went with him to Madrid and introduced him to Cánovas del Castillo,[6] then Premier of Spain. Although Cánovas was a Conservative, he felt on the Gibraltar question as deeply as the Republicans. Certain plans of a desperate character, but which really had a fair chance of success, owing to the number of Irishmen at that time in the garrison, and which would involve no action by Spain until the work had been done, when a Spanish force could be poured in, were submitted to the Prime Minister.

Cánovas listened with great attention and then said sadly that there was no object dearer to the heart of every Spaniard than the recovery of Gibraltar, but in the then state of Europe no project of the kind could be considered. Even if the fortress could be delivered into their hands, while there was no doubt that the Spanish army could defend it against all attack, the British fleet could lay waste their seacoast cities and compel Spain to surrender it to England again. Some time the opportunity would come and Gibraltar would be in Spain's hands again, but it would be useless to invite certain disaster as things then were. He referred to the old ties of friendship between Spain and Ireland, warmly thanked the Irish envoys for their offer of service and wished Ireland success in her efforts for freedom.

It was in furtherance of this policy of seeking alliances with England's enemies, which is as much the policy of Clan na Gael today, but with infinitely better prospects of success, as it was twenty-eight years ago, that Dr Carroll procured me that letter of recommendation from Senator Conover. It could not be used just then and my hands were full with the work I had already undertaken.

After arranging our plans the Secretary and I started for England, but separated at Boulogne, he going by another route and I by Folkenstone [*sic*], arranging to connect again in London. My first experience in England was characteristic of the English railway system. There was but one other occupant of the compartment I was in and before we were very far on the journey it became evident to me that he was a madman, so I travelled to London locked up with him. He was a little fellow and confined himself to half-coherent mutterings and continued shifting of his position.

The man in charge of the London district, which embraced the whole South of England, was one of those who at the Paris meeting had most strenuously opposed any alliance of any kind with the Parliamentarians, although he was not against public action which did not include that. He was a bright and clear-headed little Tipperary shoemaker named John Ryan, and he has been dead for many years. He had several tilts with Davitt in Paris, and Davitt never afterwards liked him. Davitt, in fact, developed a strong personal dislike for every Fenian who did not agree with him in this matter, and, as he scarcely made any effort to conceal it, this led to much needless friction then and later on.

Ryan had his men well in hand and my London meeting came off promptly and ended satisfactorily. I spent some days seeing the men individually or in small groups, answering questions, explaining conditions in America and hearing what they had to say. Mostly there was no discussion about the 'New Departure', but in a few cases men told me quietly and without any heat that they did not like it. One young man from Mayo was more outspoken than the rest and told me it would 'demoralise the country', and I believe he honestly thought so, but I saw him in Claremorris a few weeks later, when he was home on a vacation, riding a horse at the head of a contingent marching in to the great land meeting.

I will not go into the proceedings of the meetings in England and Scotland, or bother with the order in which they were held, because they had nothing to do with the public movement, and I will dispose of them before I touch on my trip to Ireland, although some of them took place after I had spent some time in Ireland. The two principal meetings after London were at Newcastle-on-Tyne and Glasgow. The meeting at Newcastle-on-Tyne was a convention of the North of England division of the organisation and both Davitt and the Secretary were present. Davitt was the representative of that division on the supreme government body, but, although only five men were supposed to know the rank he held (the selection being made by a committee of five and not reported to the convention), every man in the room was morally certain of it. He took a most active part in the proceedings and was evidently a general favourite. A large number of those present were Connachtmen, but many were born in England, and some were half-English in blood.

Some of those half-breeds were among the most intense men in the convention. I remember particularly one man from a small town in Lancashire who was the son of an English father and an Irish mother. He was a perfect type of an Anglo-Saxon; yellow-haired, white-skinned, blue-eyed, with a long body, short, thick legs and heavy feet, and slow and deliberate of speech. The leaders had been trying to put a stop to the stealing of rifles from the English Volunteers, practiced by some of the men, because it attracted attention to the organisation and was insignificant in results. Davitt had spoken strongly against it, and this chap stood up to reply to him. He started in by saying slowly, 'Wen I cooomed awaiay', and proceeded to demonstrate in Lancashire dialect that if every 'circle' would steal as many rifles as his the whole organisation would be armed in a given time. He was not a bit disconcerted when the vote was against him and I was told later, that he went on steadily with the work of making the British Government supply his men with rifles free of charge.

Davitt was re-elected and attended several meetings of the Executive Committee of the Council, at which I was present before I left Ireland. There was very little talk about the 'New Departure' at Newcastle and that little was in the way of explaining that it was not intended to interfere with regular Fenian work. Davitt was very clear on this point.

The thing that surprised me most in Newcastle was the good relations that existed between the North of England Fenians and some Englishmen. The convention was held in an upper room of a sort of combined hotel and public house kept by an Englishman who was a strong Radical. He knew it was an Irish meeting to be kept from the knowledge of the police and I was assured that he acted towards them with entire loyalty. He was a big, powerful Northumbrian, who knew many of them by name and asked for many absent friends.

In Edinburgh I only stopped a short time at the station to make connection with a man who came on with me to Glasgow. In Glasgow I was met by the leader of the organisation in Scotland, whom I had met in Paris, John Torley, of Duntocher, who was the superintendent of a large chemical works in that town. He died some years ago. Torley was also strongly averse to having anything to do with Parliamentary work, but favoured public action outside of that. He was born in Scotland, but was as intensely Irish as any man born on the sod could possibly be and as good a man as I have ever met. Torley had his men ready to meet me and the meeting came off satisfactorily and without any more allusion to the 'New Departure' than was necessary to explain that its advocates did not intend it to interfere in the smallest degree with Fenian work. The men there were mostly from Ulster and the northern part of Connacht.

I crossed to Ireland several times, but never went in by Dublin, because the watch for strangers was always more vigilant there than at other ports. My first trip was made by way of New Milford, where I slept a night to see if I was shadowed, and thence to Waterford, where there was practically no police surveillance at all, except the two Peelers standing by as the passengers got off the gang-plank. At other times I went from Greenock to Belfast and again by the Holyhead mail steamer to Kingstown.

Chapter 12

On the eve of the Land League in 1879

Thomas Francis Meagher[1] published in his *Irish News* some time after his arrival in New York, after his escape from Van Diemen's Land, a sketch giving his impressions of Waterford on his return from college in Belgium. It was just as if he had not gone away at all – the same shipless quays, the same half-deserted streets, the same people standing in the shop doors waiting for customers that did not come, the same policeman chewing a straw with nothing else to do – a city intended by nature for a great port with neither trade, life nor animation in it. That was in the forties, when there were more than eight millions of people in Ireland.

I landed in Waterford on 1 April 1879 (making an April fool of the British Government), and the process of decay had gone steadily on. I was thinking of that description of Meagher's when I stepped off the gang-plank of the steamer that had brought me from New Milford. There were two 'Peelers', instead of one (as I found everywhere else), a few jarveys expecting a fare, a small crowd of hungry looking young fellows looking for the job of carrying the passengers' baggage, a few people waiting to greet returning friends, but there was no crowd and no bustle, such as one seen on the arrival of a steamer at an American, an English or a French port, or even in Dublin, Belfast or Cork. The passengers were mostly from other parts of Munster, or from South Leinster, and as it was early morning, they pushed on to their homes. Waterford got nothing from them. It seemed to me that I was the only one who went to a hotel. It was a pleasure to get on an outside car again and be whirled through the deserted streets – for the old nag could trot. I suppose the sharp contrast with American cities influenced my judgment somewhat, but I never saw such a dead town as Waterford looked that day – until I struck Kilkenny. The deadness of Kilkenny appalled me.

I had no business in Waterford, except to break my journey to Dublin, and find out if I was shadowed, so after taking a room at a hotel, getting a look at the city and finding out all about the trains, I told the hotel people I had to leave for Cork at once and made a pretence of catching a Cork train, so that if the police should inquire for me they would be put on the wrong scent. I then bought a ticket for Maryborough, had supper at a little hotel there where fifteen years before I should have been well known (but I knew the place had changed hands), and got into Dublin that night.

I avoided the surveillance of the detectives by stepping out of the Kingsbridge Terminus on the entrance which faces east (they being all congregated on the south side), walked across the bridge and only hailed a jarvey when I got opposite the Royal Barracks. Then I drove to a small hotel in Upper Dominick Street, called the Royal Albert, which was frequented largely by loyalists and shoneens, and was very quiet. The place had been recommended to me for that reason.

Having no political work to do that night I paid a late visit to my own family. First I walked down Britain street to the Rotunda, where I had witnessed many a stirring scene and took a good look at Sackville street – which they still called by the old name – to see if Nelson's Pillar was still there. I had stood there as a little boy with my hand held firmly in my mother's in 1849 on the night before Queen Victoria paid her first visit to Dublin, and my mother turned away in disgust at the blaze of illuminations with some expression about the waste of money and the starving people. I had stood there again in 1853, when Victoria came a second time, to open the 'International Exhibition' that destroyed what was left of Irish industry, and shoneen Sackville street was again illuminated in her honour. I had marched in big processions through it, taken part in stormy scenes in the Rotunda, and was always proud of 'the finest street in Europe', in spite of its shoneenism, but it never looked so fine to me as on that night of 1 April, 1879, when I surveyed it in spite of England's police.

Davitt had told my family of my coming, but my arrival that night was a surprise. I expected to have little time for personal matters, so I wanted to have this visit over before getting into my political work. I was able to spend Easter Sunday at home. Davitt had dinner with us, and he and I had a long chat that evening.

I connected with Davitt and the Secretary on the morning after my arrival, got from the latter information about meetings I was to attend in various parts of the country, and had long consultations with the former on the situation, which had already begun to change, at least in the West. Before starting on any journey I first attended a meeting of the Executive Committee of the Council of the Home Organisation, with other members of that body who were within reach. Those present were a majority of the body, and Davitt was one of them. The time of the morning was taken up mainly with routine Fenian work, but there was also considerable time occupied with further discussion of the 'New Departure', about which there was still difference of opinion, and of the newspaper project, about which there was complete unanimity. There were two such meetings during my stay in Ireland and one full meeting of the Council on the eve of my departure for America in July. As the proceedings at all these meetings dealt only in part with the 'New Departure', I shall refer here only to that portion. My visits to meetings in various parts of Ireland were concerned wholly with strictly Fenian business, with only an occasional incident that had any connection with the public movement, and I shall therefore refer only to the latter.

At one of the Council meetings the final attitude of the Fenians towards the Land Movement was determined; at another the newspaper project was practically dropped and Richard Pigott left in undisputed possession of the field. I had several meetings with Davitt, Thomas Brennan and Patrick Egan, some at Davitt's lodgings in Amiens Street, others at Patrick Egan's house, with regard to the Land Movement which was springing up spontaneously in Mayo, for the purpose of properly directing it. I attended the great land meeting at Claremorris, and I had two conferences with Parnell and Davitt at Morrison's Hotel.[2] At the last of these conferences Parnell finally consented to assume the leadership of the Land Movement, and on the Sunday following went down to Westport to make his first speech in support of it. With all these matters I propose to deal briefly and without reference to their consecutive order, disposing first of the paper project.

The effort to get the *Irishman* out of Pigott's hands and to make the paper a respectable organ of sound national thought came up at the first Council meeting I attended in Dublin, and was finally disposed of at the second. Davitt had been acting as a volunteer committee of one to ascertain the actual financial condition of the *Irishman*, the price for which it might be had, the status of the mortgage which we had been told that Isaac Butt held on the paper and other matters necessary for our guidance. He had worked very assiduously and made a very full report to the meeting. Pigott, he told us, was in bad financial straits – that fact seemed to be more or less accurately known to all present – but he 'kept a stiff upper lip' in regard to price, although he did not, according to Davitt, commit himself to a definite figure. He talked loosely of £5,000, £4,000 and £3,500, but a tentative offer of £3,000 was indignantly rejected and characterised as an attempt to rob him. He talked of 'my papers' – meaning the *Irishman* and its cheap edition, the *Flag of Ireland* – as if they were great properties, and his estimate of their value was evidently founded largely on the amount of money he had been able to squeeze, through Butt, out of the rich Whig Home Rulers. As instruments of blackmail he had certainly proved them to be of considerable value, but intrinsically as business concerns they were really only worth purchasing for the purpose of getting rid of Pigott as a public scandal and danger. In all his talks, as reported by Davitt, the amount of the Butt mortgage figured as part of the value, rather than as a liability. We all believed that if he really sold the papers he would never pay a penny of this mortgage, but his talk was all of the amount he would have left after paying all his debts. He was also loaded down with debts to the Hibernian Bank, and his being able to keep afloat at all was a wonderful feat in financiering. Literally he 'lived on the interest of his debts'.

It was not Davitt who did the talking with Pigott, for they were not on speaking terms, owing to the bitter controversy over the 'New Departure', but he acted through intermediaries. Others at the meeting had also done some work in that line, and Pigott, far from keeping the matter secret, had complained to some of his friends that an attempt was being made to ruin him by forcing him to sell his papers at a great sacrifice. Some of these friends of Pigott had reached men in high positions in the organisation, so that we had Pigott's terms from several different sources, and they were the same in all cases. Pigott was an exceedingly shrewd man and had no doubt as to the source from which the purchase money would come. He could not hold his head above water much longer and was making the best fight he could for existence.

But Pigott had no sympathisers at that meeting. The wish of every man present was to get rid of him and his dishonest methods and establish a genuine Nationalist weekly organ in Dublin. They refused to temporise or to haggle, but decided to ask Davitt if he could induce Patrick Egan to foreclose the Butt mortgage for which he was said to hold a power of attorney from Mr Butt. Davitt was very sanguine of success in this and undertook the work. At the next meeting, held a short time later, he reported that Egan refused to foreclose the mortgage but that he had offered to help to induce Pigott to accept a reasonable price for the papers. The only information this meeting had as to Mr Egan's attitude in this matter was from Davitt's report, as Egan was not then a member, having been dropped on account of his refusal to stand by the decision of the Council on the question of the policy of the organisation towards Butt's Federal Home Rule Movement. Some present at the meeting had taken the trouble to get friends to sound Butt on the subject and reported that he regarded the money advanced to Pigott as hopelessly lost and would be glad to see the *Irishman* in decent hands, whether it supported his policy or not.

As Pigott's price for the *Irishman* was prohibitive and the payment of such a sum would be an inexcusable waste of money, and as no flank movement could be made on him through the Butt mortgage, the matter of obtaining control of the *Irishman* through any means was then summarily dismissed. The question of starting a wholly new paper was kept open for some time, but, owing to various causes, chief of which was the difficulty of getting an editor agreeable to all and who could live in Dublin, was finally dropped.

The matter of the attitude of the Fenians towards the 'New Departure', or rather towards the new land movement which was growing up in the West, was also finally disposed of at the second of the meetings in Dublin. The weather had much more to do with this than either Davitt or those who disagreed with him. April, a wet month in all northern climates, is particularly wet in Ireland, although the rain is usually mild. In April, 1879, the first fortnight was dry and raw and the third week almost the same. I went over a great deal of Ireland and there was not a bud to be seen on a tree or a bush until near the end of April. The country looked as it does on the immediate ever of Winter, and had nothing of Spring in it. When it began to rain it came sparingly, and the farmers were praying for more. Gradually the rain came and then there was a slow, steady fall of it until I left in July, when it looked like a particularly bad April. I rarely got a glimpse of blue sky; it was dark and leaden every day and the whole country looked dreary.

I attended many meetings in country districts, and it was never dry. Up in Glencar, above Letterkenny, in Donegal, we sat in an unoccupied farm house while the rain pattered on the roof and the dark clouds above seemed to hold a deluge. I stood with about twenty-five men in Lord Devon's demesne outside Newcastle West and we were up to the ankles in water-soaked grass. I attended a meeting of Tipperary men, most of whom are now in America, on a Sunday afternoon on the race-course about four miles from Cashel, and it drizzled most of the time. I was drenched riding on an outside car from Omagh to Strabane, had the same experience with Davitt riding from Claremorris to Ballyhaunis, and caught it on foot between Ennis and Limerick. It was rain, rain, drizzle, drizzle, and black skies nearly all the time I was in Ireland, and when I reached Paris early in July many were still wearing overcoats. I did not find an ulster a bit too warm.

After I left Ireland there came a little belated sunshine and then rainstorms and lightning finished the work of devastation. That weather made the partial famine and the famine made some kind of a land agitation inevitable. It was only a question of what form it should take and who should lead it. We had been discussing the starting of a public National movement and wrangling over the question whether it should have an agrarian feature in it or not. The forces of nature intervened and pushed the agrarian movement to the front, where it firmly established itself. This is a feature of the Irish situation in 1879 which everyone who has written of it seems to have lost sight of, yet it was the dominating and deciding factor.

At the first meeting in Dublin this situation had not fully developed, but there were ominous mutterings from Mayo. We were too busy trying to get rid of Pigott to spend much time on a subject that had been fully discussed in Paris, but by the time the second meeting came the situation had changed materially. Small meetings, all secret, had been held in Mayo, demands for counsel and assistance had come to Davitt, and Matthew Harris had seen enough in Galway to make him see that something must be done. Weeks before the first public land meeting was held at Irishtown a land movement was in the air and the toss of a penny might decide whether it was to eventuate in a more or less peaceful agitation or work wholly with shotguns and revolvers. As the supply of the latter was limited, it was very important that the decision as to what shape the movement was to take should be speedily made. Conferences had been held in Dublin which had practically made that decision, but the decision lacked authority.

Davitt brought the matter up at the second Council meeting in Dublin, but his manner was not calculated to win support. He was complaining and reproachful rather than persuasive, and he did not sufficiently explain the new situation in the West. What he now demanded was not support of the scheme discussed in Paris, but of a new one that was wholly agrarian. As his hearers were mostly townsmen, unfamiliar with conditions in Mayo, rather inclined to believe that the papers were exaggerating the situation and having a very poor opinion of the farmers as a class, they declined to touch a movement that was wholly agrarian and that seemed to them to have no promise of good in it for the National cause. But they agreed to let Davitt have a free hand, so long as his action did not interfere with National work, and to take no responsibility whatever themselves.

In the new situation this was all that could be expected, and Davitt would have been wise to accept the decision with good grace. But he did not. He spoke and acted as an injured man and his tone towards his colleagues was reproachful as if they had acted in bad faith towards him. A few practical words uttered then would have averted much of the friction that came later. Still he remained on the Council and was on the best of terms personally with all his colleagues at the meeting in July.

The land movement was thus evolved on its own lines, but, although official Fenianism had no part in it, Mayo Fenianism had the lion's share in starting it, and the rank and file of the organisation, outside of the cities, were the men who made it a power in the land. Whether this was an unmixed good or a qualified evil, for the cause of Irish Nationality, is a question about which many Nationalists differ, but there can be no question that but for the Fenians there would have been no Land League.

Chapter 13

The agitation launched at Irishtown

———————

Between the meetings I attended in various parts of the country, I returned to Dublin, where, beside the Council meetings before referred to, I had several conferences with Davitt, Thomas Brennan[1] and Patrick Egan. These were held mostly at Davitt's lodgings at 83 Amiens Street, but two of them took place at Egan's house. During the same period I had two conferences with Parnell and Davitt, both of them at Morrison's Hotel.[2] Besides this, I saw Davitt every day when both of us were in town.

As I could keep no documents or notes about me while in Ireland, I cannot fix dates as accurately as in the case of events in France, but between 1 April and the middle of July I made four trips to Paris, where I wrote reports for America, which later enabled me to keep pretty exact note of what occurred. The conferences at Davitt's lodgings began very soon after my arrival in Dublin and the basis of the discussion was always the information that Davitt had received from Mayo. I described the situation while events were still fresh in my memory in 1882, and I may quote here a little of that description from *The Land of Eire*.

> The farmers saw no prospect of getting the rent, and eviction, as well as starvation, was staring them in the face. The ghastly memories of '47[3] were revived and all Ireland was in a sullen and gloomy mood. A new generation had grown up that would not tamely submit to what their fathers had patiently borne during that terrible period, and to a great extent they were *organised*. Meetings began to be held to appeal to the

landlords for abatement of rent, and in nine cases out of ten these humble appeals were treated with contemptuous indifference. . . .

In Mayo and Sligo meetings of another kind began to be held. Groups of young men would assemble in the darkness of the night and, disguising themselves, make a violent demonstration, either against a neighbouring landlord or some weak-kneed member of their own class. This thing began to spread and would have ended in a more extensive system of Whiteboyism than had ever been seen in Ireland before. The spirit of resistance was strong, and, as sure as evictions would come landlords would be shot, the police would retaliate, and a hopeless agrarian war would be the result. Davitt saw the danger and determined to make a desperate effort to avert it. He hurried down to Mayo, pointed out the danger of the situation and induced the young men to give other methods a trial. He succeeded, and after a few preliminary gatherings the first meeting of the Land Agitation was held at Irishtown, in Mayo.

The number of people present was not nearly so large as the newspapers represented, but there were four or five thousand there, and the evidence of organisation was not lost on the authorities. The men marched in by parishes, each contingent having its leader, and took up their places according to instructions received beforehand. There was no confusion, no hurry, and the old excitement and demonstrative enthusiasm, common at Irish popular gatherings was nowhere visible. The demeanour of the men was quiet, orderly and firm, with, perhaps, a slight mixture of timidity on the part of the older men. The leaders of contingents and those who took the most active part in the proceedings were all young men and well known as staunch adherents of the National Cause. A large proportion of them had worked in England for a time, and a few had been in America. But the great majority of those present were small farmers and their sons and their relatives settled in the neighbouring towns.

The resolutions had been written beforehand by Davitt and discussed at informal meetings and social gatherings in Dublin by Patrick Egan, Thomas Brennan and others. They covered the question of Self-Government, the necessity of establishing a peasant proprietary and of an abatement of rent, pending the settlement of the Land Question.

This meeting was held on Sunday, 20 April, three weeks after my arrival. One of the men who participated in it has recently stated that Davitt had nothing to do with it,[4] but that statement is absurd. Davitt certainly was in close and direct communication with the men who organised it and made more than one journey to Mayo to advise with its promoters. I have a distinct recollection of his reading for us several letters from friends in Mayo and more than one set of very crude resolutions drafted by local men. I just as distinctly remember the discussion of the resolutions which Davitt drafted and alterations being made as a result of the discussion at Davitt's lodgings, and my recollection is that Thomas Brennan carried them down to Mayo on the eve of the meeting, at which he was one of the speakers. True, Davitt did not attend the meetings, but the passage of the resolutions which Davitt wrote, was the chief feature of the meeting, and they were the keynote of the agitation which that meeting began.

The speech of Thomas Brennan was by long odds the most important delivered at Irishtown, and Brennan went down from Dublin fresh from consultation with Davitt and very much under the spell of his influence. That the movement, as it was then understood by the men who were engaged in launching it, was not intended to be a mere Parliamentary one, was clearly indicated by Brennan's speech.

Among other things he said:

It is not on the floor of the House of Commons, but on Irish soil that the real struggle for Independence must be fought. But, as Irish Nationalists we should be glad to see the enemies of liberty obstructed and harassed, no matter where or by whom, whether it be in Westminster or Zululand, whether the attacking party be commanded by a Parnell or a Cetewayo.[5]

As Thomas Brennan has for many years resided in America it will hurt nobody to state that he was then an active Fenian and was one of the two Provincial Secretaries for Leinster. And the best proof that full freedom of action was allowed to its members by the Fenian organisation was afforded to its members by the fact that Matt Harris, a member of the Council of the organisation, was also one of the speakers at the

Irishtown meeting, and that at the next meeting of the Council in Dublin, which he attended and at which Davitt and I were present, he was neither removed from that body nor reprimanded. And among the most active organisers of the meeting were John O'Kane, then County Centre for Mayo, and Patrick W. Nally, who succeeded him in that position and was later a member of the Council.[6] As O'Kane has been many years in the United States, and poor Nally, who was one of the best men in Ireland, died in prison after having been convicted on perjured testimony on a false charge,[7] no harm can come to anybody from the mention of their connection with Fenianism.

I quote again from *The Land of Eire* regarding the effect of the Irishtown meeting:

The proceedings were reported in the Dublin papers and a howl of indignation came from the Irish Conservative and the English press. The doctrines enunciated were declared to be rank communism and the Government was urged to suppress such meetings in future. The very existence of distress was scouted and the request for a reduction of rent was pronounced to be robbery. Attention was called to it in Parliament and when some of the Irish Members pointed out the certainty of great distress, if not of actual famine, they were answered by homilies on the laziness and improvidence of the Irish people.

Lord Beaconsfield[8] talked flippantly about the Irish never providing during 'years of plenty' for bad seasons and their habit of continually appealing to the Government to remedy the results of their own 'neglect'. The sacredness of the 'rights of property' was insisted upon and the tremendous services of the Irish landlords to the tenantry, their benevolence and good nature, were extolled to the skies.'

The people read these things – they had become much more of a newspaper-reading people than in 1848 – and the natural result followed. A spirit of sullen determination not to tamely submit to a repetition of the horrors of '47 took possession of them, and they turned their thoughts to the means of procuring arms with which to resist eviction and extermination. The rain kept constantly pouring down, and as the summer advanced all lingering hopes of a fair harvest vanished. The people grew more sullen as the prospect darkened and ominous mutterings of vengeance were distinctly heard. In several districts of the West plans for the shooting of from six to twenty landlords at one stroke on the commencement of evictions were hatched, and many who afterwards took an active part in the agitation were indisposed to waste any time in a purely peaceful and legal movement.

The danger of the situation was promptly reported to Davitt and his friends, and he immediately set to work to find a remedy. He went down to his native county, examined things for himself and used all his influence with the Nationalists to restrain the people and to induce them to continue the meetings and keep their condition before the public. He had enormous difficulties to contend with, but after many discouragements and disappointments he succeeded and the agitation went on.

That this was the situation at that time I know from personal knowledge and from statements made to me by men in various parts of the country who knew the inside facts. It was then that Parnell took hold of the helm, and how he finally decided to do so will be told in another chapter.

Chapter 14

How Parnell accepted the leadership

The two days' conference with Parnell in Boulogne had given me a thorough understanding of the man and his attitude on the National Question, and I think it enabled him to fairly understand our position in America. The obstacles to an agreement were in Ireland, not in the United States, and they were not all presented by those Fenian leaders who were opposed to Parliamentary agitation. It was plain to me at Boulogne that Parnell had misgivings or doubts on two things, although he did not then give them definite expression – the possibility of a premature insurrection, on the one hand, and of an agrarian agitation drifting into demands for something else than peasant proprietary, on the other. When I met him in Dublin he went frankly into these matters and freely admitted his hesitation at assuming the leadership of the proposed new movement – for, although it was fast developing, the land movement had not yet taken definite shape.

As in the case of the Boulogne conference, the meetings with Parnell in Dublin were at his own request, conveyed to me by Davitt. The date of the first one I am not able to fix definitely, as I could keep no notes in Ireland, but my recollection is that it was on 6 April, the first Sunday after my arrival. The second one I am positive of, because it took place on the Sunday immediately preceding the Westport meeting, which was held on 8 June and the main question to be decided was whether he should attend that meeting and formally commit himself to the land movement or not. I am equally positive that both meetings with Parnell took place at Morrison's Hotel and that Davitt is utterly mistaken in placing the second one at the house of Patrick Egan,[1] as he also is on the question of a definite understanding being arrived at, so far as the three men present were concerned. I attended two meetings at Patrick Egan's house, but Parnell was not there on either occasion. Those present at both were Davitt, Thomas Brennan, Patrick Egan and I, and at the two meetings in Morrison's Hotel, the only persons present were Parnell, Davitt and I.

Davitt and I started at the same time, but did not walk together, lest we might be shadowed, the first time we met Parnell at Morrison's Hotel. It was about seven o'clock in the evening and we met in the dining-room, being his guests at supper. Thinking that if I should be recognised – a thing quite possible, as it was then only thirteen years since I had left Dublin – I suggested that we should go to a private room for our talk, as the four of us had done at Boulogne, but Parnell was decidedly against that.

'We are better here,' he said. 'If we are seen here there is no harm in it. It is a public place. But if we are in a private room it will be called a conspiracy.' I remarked to him that we met in a private room in Boulogne, but he at once reminded me that it was only a private dining-room, off the main one.

'We met in a hotel room in London,' he said, referring to the meeting with Dr Carroll, 'and we were overheard. Here nobody can hear us.'

Davitt and I at once recognised that this was the commonsense view and we remained in the dining-room. My anxiety was to prevent harm coming to Parnell through being seen with me, an outlaw, but in this, as in so many other matters at that time, his judgement was sound.

Davitt wanted my help to secure Parnell for leader of the new movement. He had himself made some impression on him and the Boulogne conference had done a good deal towards bringing him round, but things in Ireland had already changed a good deal and the movement for which Davitt now wanted his aid was an agrarian one, instead of the one planned in the 'New Departure'. The Irishtown meeting had not yet been held, but the bad conditions in the West and the threats of disturbances had been made known to him. He had practically made up his mind to go into the movement if it should be carried out on the lines we had discussed in Boulogne, but the changed situation required careful handling and he could not possibly foresee that Davitt and his friends would be able to keep the Mayo men so well in hand as they afterwards demonstrated their ability to do. He could see his way to arrive at an understanding with the Fenians if they were willing, but at that time (6 April) they had not yet made their final decision. Without such an understanding and without something more definite than was yet forthcoming from the West he refused to undertake the work, but showed the keenest interest in the situation and freely gave us advice.

I did not join Davitt in asking Parnell to commit himself to a purely agrarian movement, but Davitt pleaded hard with him. My talk was all in favour of the larger programme that had been up to then discussed and I had still some hopes of securing the definite agreement with the Fenians which Parnell wanted, on all except the Parliamentary feature. On that I knew that agreement would be impossible. I informed Parnell that their final answer could not be obtained for some weeks, but that there was no doubt as to the attitude of the men in America.

That first meeting at Morrison's Hotel had nothing whatever formal about it. It was simply a confidential chat about the situation – already becoming more than usually interesting – between three men. There was nobody sitting at any table near us, and for most of the time the dining-room was entirely vacant except for the coming and going of the waiters and they were out of earshot, except while serving us.

When the political talk was over we drifted into other subjects. Parnell asked me no questions whatever about Fenianism except as to the attitude of the leaders towards the subject we were discussing and the proportion of farmers and farm labourers among its membership. I was not then able to answer him on the latter point, as I had not yet seen anything of the country, and Davitt's knowledge of it was mainly confined to the West, where there were many small farmers and a few 'strong' ones in the Fenian ranks. Later I found a goodly proportion of farmers in the organisation in Ulster, Connacht and Munster, but hardly any in Leinster.

I asked Parnell about his American grandfather, Commodore Stewart,[2] and found he knew nothing of his career except what he had heard from his mother. He was somewhat better informed about his father's people, but I found he had never heard that a distinguished ancestor, or relative, had written a book in defence of the Irish Catholics.[3] And I repeat, notwithstanding some recent denials of the fact, that, while he had a very fair general idea of the chief events in Ireland since 1782, and knew that there were wars and colonisations in the time of Elizabeth, James the First, Cromwell and William of Orange, he was very ignorant of Irish history. But about the then condition of Ireland he was thoroughly and minutely informed.

Parnell asked me how I proposed to spend my time in the intervals of work, supposing that meetings would probably be far apart. He had heard me say that I had tramped in early youth over some of the Wicklow mountains and told me he had a hunting lodge at Lugnaquilla,[4] where he would be very glad to have me spend a few days with him. There, he said, we could have ample opportunity to talk, and he left no room for doubt that he was anxious for more talk with me. He was quite frank, as he was at Boulogne, concealed nothing on his own part and asked no information that was not necessary to the proper understanding of the subject under discussion. The description of him as a cautious and taciturn Constitutionalist 'pumping' a loquacious Fenian was the invention of one of the men who 'flung Parnell to the English wolves'. It was intended to discredit the policy which Parnell and the Fenian had agreed on, and to which the Fenian remained loyal until Parnell was laid in Glasnevin.

I thanked Parnell for the invitation but told him that the itinerary arranged for me would keep me 'on the jump' all the time and leave no chance for pleasure of that kind. As a matter of fact, during the three and a half months I spent in Ireland I saw none of the sights that tourists visit, except a glimpse of Loch Erne on my way from Enniskillen to Bundoran. I went from Belfast to Derry and back, and did not see the Giants' Causeway. I was in Newcastle West and Macroom, but did not see either Killarney or Glengariff,[5] and during the same time I made only two social calls, one on P. J. Smyth[6] and the other on Dr Sigerson.[7]

The person who supplied the fanciful account of my relations with Parnell to Mr Barry O'Brien[8] drew very largely on an imagination highly coloured by personal prejudice and by the differences growing out of the Parnell split. As there was nobody present at either interview but Parnell, Davitt and I, and Mr O'Brien did not get the information directly or indirectly from me, the perverted version must have been supplied by someone who heard the story from Davitt and twisted it to suit the anti-Parnellite claim that the Parliamentary Party was not bound in any way to follow certain lines. Davitt's denial of a definite understanding I will deal with later.

But no understanding was reached at that first meeting at Morrison's except that the three should meet again, after the Fenian leaders should have met and the situation should have cleared in Mayo. When the second meeting between Parnell, Davitt and myself was held on the evening of 1 June 1879, the whole situation had cleared and things had begun to take more definite shape. The Irishtown meeting had been held, and during the forty days that had since elapsed much had happened. The continued rains had rendered certain the prevalence of widespread distress. Davitt had been down to Mayo and conferred with the people, I had visited various places in all of the four provinces, seen conditions for myself, and felt the pulse of the men, and the Fenians had finally decided to leave their members entire liberty of action. The 'New Departure' as a concrete proposition had been dropped or jostled out of the way, as agrarian agitation was springing up spontaneously in Mayo with some planks borrowed from it, and the question that confronted us was, could it be kept within rational channels, developed into a great, disciplined National Movement and supplied with a capable, clear-headed and resolute leader?

Davitt, always a sanguine man, except during brief intervals of depression, was very confident of success if we could only get the leader, and at that time he had full faith in Parnell. I don't think he had then any notion that he could himself be the titular leader, though I saw very clear and convincing evidence that in a short time he developed the belief that he was 'the power behind the throne' – the driving force which kept the movement going – and that at a very early stage he resented Parnell's quiet and silent, but very emphatic refusal to be a mere figurehead. This state of feeling grew more intense in both men as time went on and was the real cause of the Split,[9] but in June, 1879, Davitt was a firm believer in the absolute necessity of having Parnell as leader.

After my two previous interviews with Parnell and with my knowledge of existing conditions and of men then available, I had arrived at the conclusion that no other leader than Parnell was possible. There was no other man among the Members of Parliament or known in the public life of Ireland, who was at all fit, and, although some of the Fenians had greater intellect and a better education, they had no training in public life. Davitt was developing great ability as an agitator and leader of men, but his impetuous temperament, and lack of tact, to say nothing of his social standing, made him impossible. That he became the chief driving force in the early years of the agitation is conceded by everyone who knows anything of its inside history, but looking back over the twenty-seven years that have elapsed since that conference in Dawson Street, I am as strongly convinced now as I was then that Parnell was the only possible leader.

I am also satisfied that had Davitt attempted to lead the movement himself, it would have been a convulsion, filled perhaps with tragedies that would have been historic, but ending in speedy failure. I am aware of all the fine things said about Democracy, and I am a Democrat of an extreme type. I know I shall be told that Napoleons in embryo are as plenty as blackberries, and that the bones of 'mute inglorious Miltons' and 'Cromwells guiltless of their country's blood' are to be found in every country churchyard. I don't deny it, but I have seen red Irish setters of purest blood reared in American cities and untrained that were absolutely useless to the sportsman, and even carpenters, shoemakers, tailors and printers are not produced without long and careful training. There is more latent political talent in Ireland than perhaps in any other country under the sun – Americans freely admit that, even if they resent it – but the Irish are still clansmen who follow their chief.

I am speaking of the Ireland of 1879 when I say that Parnell was the only possible leader of the Land League. Let any thinking man look back over the years that have elapsed since he fell, and whether he may claim that his deposition was a cruel necessity or regard it as a craven and suicidal surrender to England, as I do, he cannot deny the utter barrenness and sterility of leadership which have characterised Ireland ever since. Napoleons, Hannibals, Oisins, Shakespeares, Miltons, and

O'Connells may be lying around in embryo all the time, but they are only developed once in a generation or so. It was so with Parnell, although he was not really a great man.

Before starting to have the final talk with Parnell on that Sunday evening in June, 1879, Davitt and I had a long conference and came to a clear understanding as to the conditions we should propose and the promises we should make. Neither of us could speak for the whole Fenian movement, but both combined were empowered to speak for a very large number of Fenians. Davitt for large groups and individual local leaders in the West of Ireland, in the North of England, and a few in Dublin, and I for practically all the organised Nationalists in America. We were to let him know the exact position of the Fenians in Ireland – that as an organisation they would hold aloof, but that every individual Fenian was free to act, so long as his action was not inconsistent with the principles or hostile to the interests of Fenianism. We were free to promise him our individual help within our respective 'spheres of influence', provided he agreed to our terms.

Davitt had committed himself so completely to the land agitation that he was ready to take Parnell without exacting any terms except a general acceptance of the Irishtown resolutions,[10] but I was in a different position and insisted on clear and definite conditions, which I was perfectly sure that Parnell would readily accept. I was thinking of the politicians who would flock to the movement after it became popular and who might imitate Sadleir and the 'Brass Band', who wrecked the Tenant League in the fifties.[11] I had also to think of the men in America who trusted me and I dared not face them with an admission that I had pledged their support without exacting the clearest and most explicit understanding as to the aims, objects and limitations of the movement.

We met Parnell, stated our conditions, heard others from him that were just as explicit and we reached an agreement. These and the sequel will be told in another chapter.

NOTES AND ANSWERS

In the last article on 'Davitt and the Fenians', published a fortnight ago, it was stated that Matthew Harris, of Ballinasloe, made a speech at the initial meeting of the Land Movement at Irishtown, County Mayo on 20 April 1879. This was an error. It was at Miltown, the third meeting of the series, held on 15 June that Harris made his first speech in the land agitation, but that was previous to the Council meeting in Dublin, referred to in the last article, at which he met Davitt and his fellow-Fenians – so that the rest of the reference to Matthew Harris was correct.

Chapter 15

Conditions which Parnell agreed to

At the conference with Parnell at Morrison's Hotel on Sunday, 1 June 1879, Davitt and I fully recognised that we must either reach a definite agreement or drop the negotiations for good. The talk was therefore clearer and more definite than at any previous meeting. We had 'come down to hard pan' at last, and must decide once for all whether there was to be a partnership or not.

The action of the Fenians was fully explained to Parnell. As an organisation they would do nothing, but every individual member was left free to go into the public movement if he thought proper, provided his action was not antagonistic to the principles or interests of Fenianism. Davitt and I were not there in the capacity of representatives of the Fenian organisation and we had no authority to speak for it, much less to make a bargain or treaty in its name. At Boulogne I was one of two representatives of the supreme authority of the Irish Revolutionary organisation at home and abroad, but on account of the action of the men at home that status no longer existed. Parnell was made fully aware of all this, but was also informed that Davitt and I knew we could speak for large bodies of Fenians, Davitt in Ireland and I in America. He had to take our word for this and he did. He knew he was dealing with two individual men, not with envoys or ambassadors, just as we knew that he was speaking merely as an individual and not as the representative of any organised body of men, either in Parliament or out of it. He had nothing beyond moral certainty, if he even had that, that we could 'deliver the goods', just as Davitt and I had no more than our opinion as to Parnell's ability to carry out any agreement that might be made.

This was the exact situation, and it explains some of the evidence before the Commission[1] and all of the quibbling and prevarication that have been indulged in since in regard to Parnell's relations with the Fenians. We arrived at an agreement, clear, definite and precise, so far as vital political principles were concerned, but utterly ignoring details. It was a personal agreement between Charles Stewart Parnell, Michael Davitt and John Devoy, as to the course that all three would follow in connection with the public agitation, and the shape and character we would endeavour to give it. On that agreement Parnell undertook to take the leadership of the movement and Davitt and I pledged ourselves to support him. I distinctly stipulated that if any change should be made, either in the leadership or the programme, without the consent of those for whom I undertook to speak, the agreement would at once come to an end. It could not with safety be reduced to writing and was therefore only verbal, but it was none the less binding on all three. And, as it only covered a few important points, there was little danger of any of its terms being forgotten.

The agreement entered into was in substance as follows:

First: That in the conduct of the public movement, so far as Parnell and Davitt could influence it, there should not be anything said or done to impair the vitality of the Fenian movement or to discredit its ideal of complete National Independence, to be secured by the eventual use of physical force.

Second: that the demand for Self-Government should not for the present be publicly defined, but that nothing short of a National Parliament with power over all vital National interests and an Executive responsible to it should be accepted.

Third: That the settlement of the Land Question to be demanded should be the establishment of a peasant proprietary to be reached by compulsory purchase.

Fourth: That the Irish Members of Parliament elected through the public movement should form an absolutely independent party, asking and accepting no places, salaried or honorary, under the English Government, either for themselves, their constituents or anyone else.

I do not claim that the agreement was put in this exact form, or in these words, but I assert that all the points mentioned above were agreed to in words having precisely the same meaning, and in the same order as I have given them. On Parnell's acceptance of them Davitt and I agreed that, so far as we could influence the action of the Fenians in Ireland and America, there should be no cessation whatever in the work of organisation and preparation for armed revolution, but that there should be no attempt at insurrection until the new programme should have had a fair trial. This promise was easily made because we knew that, as conditions then were, no insurrection would have a ghost of a chance for several years to come and that those Fenian leaders who differed with us did not contemplate a resort to force until conditions should have greatly improved and a clear opportunity should present itself.

Parnell discussed the terms fully and freely. His solicitude was mainly on two points. He wanted the country to have a fair chance of having an intelligent policy presented to it and organising itself, and he feared that hot-headed and impulsive men might force a premature crisis. He felt pretty sure that there would be no attempt at actual insurrection, but he knew that, imprudent and inflammatory speeches, or the deliberate provocation of the Government's agents in carrying out evictions, suppressing meetings and enforcing coercion, might at any time provoke riots and attempts at retaliation that would offer the excuse for massacres of the unarmed people and the stamping out of the movement before it could accomplish anything or obtain sufficient hold on the country.

I say 'the unarmed people' because I found that Parnell attached great importance to the question of armament. Later on I shall deal with a plan he had for organised resistance to eviction which would amount to guerrilla warfare, but which was not carried out, because the necessary arms were not to be had. It was not that he had any objection to the use of physical force, but his anxiety to apply the means at hand to the solution of the problem immediately confronting him that made him so careful at this meeting.

A great deal has been said about a saying of Parnell's that 'the greatest mistake the Fenians made was to fight', as if he intended to disparage them. He said something like that at this meeting in Morrison's Hotel in June, 1879, and I immediately told him I was in full agreement with him and that he would find every thoughtful Fenian of the same mind. Of course, what Parnell meant was to fight at the wrong time and with ridiculously inadequate means of fighting. But he believed in fighting men and he left no doubt on my mind that he based his hope of success at that time on the assurance we gave him of the support of large numbers of Fenians. And it was not the organised Fenians whose imprudence he feared, but the unorganised and untrained portion of the people.

The first plank in the agreement was by long odds the most important, because, no matter what the other terms might be, no Fenian could take part in the movement except on that condition. And, as Ireland then was, and as Irish organisations in America then were, the movement would have amounted to nothing without the help of large numbers of Fenians in Ireland and without the vigorous support given it by the Clan na Gael in America. Parnell had no hesitation in agreeing to it and wasted no time in discussing it.

The second plank was intended to avoid clashes between Fenians, who believed in Total Separation, Repealers, who were not wholly extinct in Ireland at that time, and Federal Home Rulers who might favour the land programme and be swept into the current. I did not believe that England would grant Home Rule on a peaceful demand and I wanted to leave the definition open until the necessity for defining it should arise. But I did believe that some kind of representative county government might be conceded in the hope of allaying the National demand and that we could use it to strengthen our position. Parnell did not haggle over that, any more than the first plank.

It was over the third plank that most of the discussion took place, but not at all for the reasons those familiar with public controversies that took place later on might suppose. Parnell believed in peasant proprietary: it was his ideal solution, and, as he did not think a successful revolution probable in the immediate future, he wanted it reached through purchase. He was not so sure that compulsory purchase was

likely to be conceded within any reasonable time, but he thought many
of the landlords would agree to sell if the machinery and the funds were
provided. His fear was that politicians and lawyers might get hold of the
movement and put forward a less satisfactory settlement.

Davitt's anxiety was on the same score. He, too, believed in peasant
proprietary, but was only a recent convert. He had talked in America of
'the land for the people' but had never clearly defined his plan. He had
not at that time read 'Progress and Poverty' and had never heard of
Henry George.[2] Neither had he read, or heard of, James Fintan Lalor[3]
and the term 'land nationalisation' was not in his vocabulary. I believed
in peasant proprietary as a means of breaking up the big estates and
destroying the power of England's landlord garrison. We all were agreed
on peasant proprietary as the thing to be demanded and only wanted to
make the plank rigid, so that neither trimming politician nor place-
hunting lawyer might be able to change it to something less. I am safe in
saying that I was the only one of the three who looked to a more extreme
settlement later on, but, as I had said in the resolutions at Davitt's New
York meeting in 1878, that solution must wait for an Irish Republic.

The last plank was agreed to as a matter of course. Parnell was
already acting on it and it was his own policy. Davitt was not bothering
himself much at that time about what might be done in Parliament. His
mind was filled with the work to be done on the soil of Ireland and
among the Irish in America. He and I agreed to the plank as a necessity
of the situation, but Davitt seemed to me at that time to be as strongly as
I was myself in favour of a policy looking to eventual withdrawal from
Parliament.

When this agreement was finally arrived at Davitt and I pledged our
words to Parnell that we would stand by him so long as he stood by that
programme. He then agreed to attend the meeting at Westport on the
following Sunday and commit himself formally to the movement. He
did so and in his speech told the people to 'keep a firm grip of their
holdings', which really gave the movement its watchword. Archbishop
MacHale[4] issued his famous fulmination against the agitation[5] a few
days before the meeting at Westport and Davitt, fearing it might deter
Parnell, called on him, in some anxiety as to the course he might take,

but Parnell was not in the least disturbed and assured Davitt that he would keep his word. I did not see Parnell again in Ireland, but met him frequently in America.

*

I shall deal at the proper time with statements that have been made that Parnell made no compact and arrived at no understanding with me, or anyone else representing the Fenians or the Clan na Gael. I will only say here that Parnell's whole policy was based on the lines of that agreement, that if he did not promise to carry it out he must have made a very accurate guess as to what would win the Clan na Gael's support, and that that support was given him because of any report that he had agreed to the policy. The contradiction was never made until after Parnell's death. Twice during his lifetime, and in defence of his policy, I made pointed public allusion to the existence of the compact, and the challenge was not taken up, nor did Parnell complain of it. On more than one occasion when the policy was assailed Parnell asked my help, through a Member of Parliament who was in his confidence, and the attempt to drive him from the leadership and wreck the policy was completely defeated through the influence of the Clan na Gael in the American Land League. And he appealed again in his last desperate fight which ended in his overthrow and the disruption of the movement.

Chapter 16

Why the Fenians were hostile to Sullivan

A short time after the last interview with Parnell an incident occurred which threw a peculiar light on some of the forces at work in Irish public life at that period and which have continued to exist up to the present. Few people at the present day can understand the bitterness of the hostility of the Fenians to A. M. Sullivan,[1] the editor of the Dublin *Nation*, but in 1879 it was well understood. Mr Sullivan in the earlier days of Fenianism had gone on a yachting tour around the southern coast of Ireland and had knocked up against some Fenians. Stephens had tried to enlist him in the movement and had failed, but it seemed natural to some of those he met to speak freely to the editor of the *Nation*, and they informed him, he said, that his name and that of William Smith O'Brien[2] had been used by somebody to induce them to join the movement.

As Mr Sullivan did not name those who spoke to him, it was not possible to verify his statement, but on going back to Dublin he wrote a letter to William Smith O'Brien telling him his name was being used to inveigle young men into a secret society and asking him to say that this use of his name was unauthorised. O'Brien did so, and then Mr Sullivan published his own letter and O'Brien's reply in the *Nation*, with an article condemning the alleged action of the men he accused. This publication may or may not have been the first information received of the work then going on in the South of Ireland; but whether it preceded that given by Sullivan 'Goula'[3], or what was sent to the Castle by Archdeacon O'Sullivan, of Kenmare,[4] through a gross abuse of the confessional, or came later, makes little difference. It was certainly of much more importance than either, for it appeared in a Nationalist paper with a great name, contained a condemnation by one of the most popular leaders of the Young Ireland movement and conveyed the information that the work of spreading a secret, illegal society, was going on in other parts of Munster, as well as Kerry. It was a foul blow aimed at a leader who could not defend himself, because a denial that he had used O'Brien's or Sullivan's name would be an admission that he was engaged in illegal work in Ireland when he was supposed to be living abroad. The article did not name Stephens, but clearly indicted him, and it accused him of being an untruthful and dishonourable man. This exposure undoubtedly forced the hand of the Government and the arrest and trial of O'Donovan Rossa and the other Phoenix men in 1858 was a natural result. The fact that the *Nation* helped to raise the 'Fair Trial Fund' which defended the prisoners did not in the least allay the indignation of thousands of men who were not yet Fenians against Mr Sullivan.

This was intensified by the conflict between the 'Moderates' and the physical force men over the control of the funeral of Terence Bellew McManus[5] in 1861, which resulted in a complete victory for the Fenians. They managed the funeral and obtained control of a public meeting in the Rotunda, at which the delegates who had brought the body of McManus from America were to speak. The 'Moderates' had planned to start at that meeting a public organisation on their own lines but the Fenians captured the meeting and had a large number of their own men appointed on the committee. In the next issue of the *Nation* this was denounced and the list of the committee printed with the names of those whom Mr Sullivan suspected of being Fenians printed in Italics and with a footnote explaining that the names in Italics were 'friends of the Fenian delegates'. It was the enmity caused by these actions of Mr Sullivan which caused a meeting in the Rotunda to be broken up in 1863, because The O'Donoghue,[6] in his speech, referred to him as 'my esteemed friend, Mr Sullivan', and which led to many other stormy scenes of that period.

Mr Sullivan had, to a considerable extent, lived down this prejudice; he had joined in the demonstrations of protest against the hanging of the men in Manchester, had fought side by side with Fenians for

John Martin in the Longford election,[7] and in 1879 it was mainly the older Fenians who still hated him. He was one of the Members of Parliament for Louth and, being a great temperance man, was a strong advocate of the Sunday Closing Bill then before the House of Commons, and which referred to Ireland only. The liquor dealers were doing their utmost to defeat the Bill and thought they could make use of the Fenian hostility against Mr Sullivan to some advantage. A man named O'Connor, who had come into Dublin from the Bog of Allen as a 'grocer's curate' and had grown to be a wealthy liquor dealer, was then President of the Liquor Dealers' Association and was conducting their campaign against the Bill. O'Connor was afterwards Member of Parliament for one of the divisions of Kerry, selected for some inscrutable reason. His manners may have mended from long residence in Dublin, but I was assured by Matt Slattery of Cork Hill that when he was an apprentice to an uncle of his in Winetavern Street he was known by an elegant nickname suggested by his habit of using the cuff of his coat as a pocket handkerchief.

Davitt learned that this man O'Connor had undertaken to use the Fenians in most unwarrantable way against Mr Sullivan. The parish priest of a village about twelve miles from Dundalk, the name of which I forget, had invited Mr Sullivan to deliver a lecture for the benefit of a Catholic school and the future member for Kerry conceived the brilliant idea, or some one put it into his head, that if this meeting in Sullivan's own constituency could be broken up it would discredit him and help to beat the Sunday Closing Bill. Of course, the idea was utterly stupid, and if violence had occurred at the meeting it would have proved to be a strong argument in favour of the Bill, instead of against it. There was a Dundalk man then living in Dublin who had been a Fenian, but was strongly suspected by Davitt and others of being a British spy. He was certainly an unprincipled fellow, and I found that none of the Dublin Fenians had any use for him. I shall call him M., as that was the initial of his name. O'Connor, the future Home Rule MP, gave this fellow ten pounds and sent him to Dundalk to organise a Fenian demonstration against Sullivan at the lecture in the Catholic church.

M. went to Dundalk, said nothing at all about the liquor dealers or the Sunday Closing Bill, but a great deal about Sullivan's attacks on the

Fenians and got the local men to promise to break up the meeting. Davitt told me all about it and I immediately made up my mind to go to Dundalk and try to stop the bad work. Davitt told me there was no use in his going, first because Haire, the 'County Centre' (now dead), did not like him, and secondly, because of his bad relations with a Dublin liquor dealer who was a Fenian. I went to the Secretary of the Fenian organisation, told him the story, and he at once promised to help me out to the utmost of his ability. A few hours' investigation convinced him that the plot was fully hatched and that the Dundalk men were going blindfold into the trap. The Secretary and I started at once for Dundalk and set to work. His part was chiefly introducing me to Haire and telling him that I was the American envoy, having authority from the Council to visit the organisation.

I found Haire to be a splendid fellow, and his men, who numbered several hundred, about as fine types physically as I had met in Ireland. Haire was a powerful man, of fine physique, about five feet ten inches in height, with clear-cut features that were almost handsome, steel grey eyes that looked through you when he was animated, but were very quiet in repose. He had several scars on his head and I learned that he had got them all in fights with the Ribbonmen[8] whom he had practically driven out of Louth because of an old feud started by them, which no longer exists, but was at one time very bitter in Ulster and Connacht. He was a well-to-do man in the carting business and had absolute command over his men. He was able to collect them at short notice for my inspection, and I said nothing of the Sullivan matter until he, the Secretary and myself were alone.

H. was at first disinclined to believe that M. was capable of such a dirty trick, but the Secretary assured him he had investigated the case and that there could be no doubt about it. Then Haire was very angry at being made a tool of, but he had the old Fenian hatred of Sullivan and thought it very hard to let him make a speech in the county without some expression of opposition. I told him that a lecture in a Catholic church was not likely to be used by Mr Sullivan for a political speech, but he shook his head. Finally, I got him to agree to a compromise. I proposed to him to take four or five of his best men with him to the lecture, that they should sit quietly during the proceedings and only act in case Sullivan should say something about his course in Parliament. Then they were to make a protest, which I drafted for them, against using a meeting held for a charitable purpose in a Catholic church for a political purpose and challenging Mr Sullivan to speak at a public meeting of his constituents where all would be free to ask him questions. Haire thought this was fair and agreed to it. Then I said too much and nearly spoiled all.

I said to Haire, 'Besides, it would be a most imprudent thing for the few men you could bring from Dundalk, for there will surely be a big crowd of farmers' sons there who would be more than a match for them.'

The grey eyes flashed fire, he clapped his right hand on my knee, holding it in a grip of steel, and leaning over till his face was close to mine, he said: 'See here, young fellow; any twenty men we'd take out of this town could bate all the bloody farmers in the County Louth. Do you understand that?'

I did understand it. I had seen a good many of his men and I had no doubt of their ability to give a good account of themselves in any kind of a fight, but it would be deplorable if these men who had sworn to fight for Ireland should be brought to disgrace and dishonour by fighting the battle of the sordid and unpatriotic Dublin liquor dealers. The 'fight-ing man' won't tolerate doubts of its capacity to fight or imputations on its courage, and my thoughtless remark had aroused the fighting spirit in Haire. It took me some time to recover the ground I had lost and he gave me his word that he would carry out the compromise plan before mentioned.

Having read in reports of elections of riotous scenes in Dundalk where mobs of working men had swept all before them in the interest of Philip Callan,[9] almost every time he ran for Parliament, and hearing that Haire had always supported him, I broached the subject to him after we had settled the Sullivan matter. I asked him how it was that Dundalk Nationalists could support a man who was notoriously corrupt and who was evidently looking for a place from the British Government. 'Because when he had money,' said Haire, 'he spent it like a man, among the boys in this town where he was reared. He is hard up now and they are not going to go back on him. Besides, he is as good as any of the rest of them.' There was no use arguing against this spirit of loyalty to a local chief, which was intensified by sympathy with his misfortunes. It was like arguing with a Kerryman of the old generation against The O'Donoghue – 'the gifted young Chieftain of the Glens'. I said to Haire: 'But doesn't Callan's whole action show that he is looking for a job?'

'I'd be glad to see the poor fellow get a job,' was his simple reply, and I had to give it up. I learned later that Phil. Callan had been a Fenian in his younger days, and being a good deal of a fighting man, the Dundalk men clung to the belief that he was still ready to fight for Ireland if the chance should come. From all I heard I was satisfied that Callan began by being an honest Nationalist, but was driven by his financial necessities, which were the result of his spendthrift habits, into equivocal courses. And, looking backward over the intervening years, I am inclined to rate him as high as many men of the Parliamentary Party who have taken no jobs from the British Government, but have no real claim to be called Nationalists.

The Secretary and I returned to Dublin, and at the earliest possible moment I informed Davitt of the result of the trip to Dundalk. He at once saw T. D. Sullivan,[10] who promised to inform his brother. 'Ah Im,' as he called him, of the fact that he need not fear any trouble. I asked Davitt to particularly request Mr Sullivan not to ask any police assistance, as it would be wholly unnecessary.

After visiting other parts of the country and getting back to Dublin I learned the final result of our mission to Dundalk. Haire brought a dozen men on two jaunting cars to the lecture, intending to keep his word with me, sit quietly in the church during Mr Sullivan's talk and only read the protest in the event of any political allusion being made. But M. was determined to earn his £10 and insisted on being one of the party. He was allowed to go on a promise that he would keep quiet, but no sooner had Mr Sullivan begun to speak than he shouted 'Goula'. That was the nickname of the Kerry informer on 1858, and for a time many of the Fenians had applied it to Mr Sullivan, but they had long ceased to do so. M. had managed to repeat the epithet three or four times, in spite of his companions' efforts to retrain him, when the parish priest, a tall and very stalwart man, strode down the middle aisle, and taking him by the scruff of the neck, flung him out. Then he turned to the other Dundalk men and ordered them out. Having been put hopelessly in the wrong by the blackguard who had taken Dirty Cuff O'Connor's bribe money, and having a natural objection to disgracing themselves in a Catholic church, they meekly obeyed. I heard that they punished M. badly for his misconduct and later he came to America, where he died.

When I met A. M. Sullivan in New York some years later, he expressed gratified surprise at finding me a member of the Land League. He was still more surprised when I told him I had come in 'on the ground floor' before he had made up his mind to join it. When he stood on the platform of the Cooper Institute facing an audience largely composed of old Fenians, he looked decidedly nervous at first, his memory doubtless going back to stormy scenes in the Rotunda. But the hearty welcome he received soon put him at his ease. And his surprise at being well received by old Fenians was no greater than theirs at finding a calm speaker standing erect without gesticulation, instead of the swaying figure, swinging arms and West Cork accent – described by Con. O'Mahony as 'like the milling of the waves on the seashore' – which they remembered so well in Ireland. But Sullivan was tolerated for the good of the cause rather than for any belief in his power for good. His oratory was not the kind that warms Irishmen and his tour accomplished nothing.

Chapter 17

The great Claremorris land meeting

The Land Meeting held at Claremorris, County Mayo, on Sunday, 13 July 1879, was the fourth of the series, and was the largest of the four. It was my luck to be able to attend it, or rather a portion of it, as a spectator, but I had some difficulty in doing so.

The differences of opinion about O'Connor Power between Davitt and the other Nationalists – even those who agreed with him on the Land Question – influenced nearly everything done at that time, and it caused efforts to be made to keep me from going to Claremorris. Davitt bitterly resented any hint of his undue friendship for Power, even when made jocularly, but his partiality for him kept cropping up continually. Power was then one of the two members of Parliament for Mayo; he had been elected because the Mayo Fenians, the strongest force in the county, had fought for him and borne down all opposition, and his chance of winning at the next election depended entirely on the support of the men of the organisation. The man at the head of the Mayo organisation, John O'Kane, was a supporter of Power and had not, I was told, been informed that the leaders of the organisation were opposed to Power's re-election. He thought that in supporting Power he was carrying out the wishes of the leaders.

A County Convention of the Fenians of Mayo was to take place in Claremorris on that Sunday under cover of the big land meeting and very much would depend on what would be said and done there, as well as on the men elected to office. A similar County Convention was to take place on the same day in Galway, and each had to be attended by a representative from Headquarters, as well as, if possible, by a man from

America. General Millen[1] had recently been sent over in a military capacity, and one of us was to go to each of the two meetings.

Davitt told me he thought it would be dangerous for me to go to Claremorris, on account of the crowd, the extra police, the reporters and the public men who would be there. Some of them might recognise me, whereas Millen was not so well known and if recognised, they could not put him in prison, as they would me if they caught me. It was, therefore, he said, better for me to go to Galway, where there was no crowd and let Millen go to Claremorris.

At first I did not suspect that Davitt had any other reason for keeping me away than those he mentioned, and I merely argued that his fears were groundless. I also told him frankly that I wanted to feel the pulse of the Mayo men about O'Connor Power, and that I wished to see one land meeting before returning to America. I thought I had succeeded in convincing him, and I went to the Secretary, who made arrangements as to where each of us from America was to go.

On Saturday morning, a relative of mine met Davitt at the Broadstone Terminus as he was starting for Claremorris, and brought me the urgent message that I ought not under any circumstances to go there. The reason was the old one, that I was in danger of arrest, but was urged with greater force, as if he had some new evidence. I got the message in less than an hour, but it did not swerve me a bit from my purpose of going. The arrangements for my going had already been made and the local men notified, and all would be upset if I should fail to turn up.

A few hours later as I was waiting for my own train, which was also to convey Millen as far as Athlone, on his way to Galway, I saw Thomas Brennan[2] on the platform at the Broadstone. The Secretary was also there, but none of the four of us spoke to the other in the presence of the strangers and the police on duty. Mr Brennan passed close to me and in a low voice told me to step for a moment into a private place where he could have a word with me. I went as directed, and he said to me:

'John, I don't think you ought to go to Claremorris. You are in danger of arrest.

I am in danger of arrest every hour of the twenty-four,' I replied, 'and I'll be in no more danger in Claremorris than anywhere else.'

'I think you're mistaken,' he said, 'there are two detectives on the platform now.'

'There are two "Peelers", or two detectives, at every railroad station in Ireland, and there's nothing unusual in those two fellows being here,' I replied. 'I'm going to Claremorris and I'll take my chances of arrest.'

Brennan bade me good-bye somewhat sadly, as if he did not expect to see me again, and I started for the West.

Arrived at Claremorris I saw two tall strapping 'Peelers' standing in a sort of yard outside the station and a group of young fellows stood near them, as if watching for somebody. It was not my habit to have friends wait for me at a railroad station and recognise me in the presence of the police, and none of them had ever done it before, so I did not expect that anyone would be waiting for me. I was walking past the young men when one of them stepped up to me and within three feet of the police-men asked me: 'Are you Misther Doyle?'

That was the name I was to take in Claremorris, so I promptly said 'No'.

As I knew the 'Peelers' had heard and I saw they were looking at me, I walked right up to them and said: 'Would you be kind enough to tell me which is the best hotel in this town?'

'Well,' answered one of the constabulary-men, 'there's two, and they're both about the same. If there's any choice between them it's in favour of the one next the barrack. We'll be going down in a minute and if you wait we'll show it to you.'

I thanked them, waited and walked into Claremorris in the company of the two policemen. I knew, from experience while 'on my keeping' in 1865–6, that my action had disarmed the suspicion aroused by the imprudence of my friends and would cause the latter to give me a wide berth during the evening, which was what I wanted.

I wore a suit of Irish tweed and carried a frieze overcoat on my arm, my accent was home-made and there was nothing about me to suggest the returned Irish-American. But I had to do something to account for my arrival there on a Saturday evening on the eve of a land meeting: so I told the policemen confidentially that I was a correspondent of the *Times*, sent to report the meeting. I felt sure from their manner that they did not like me any the better for this announcement, as they looked like farmers' sons, but they were very polite during the rest of my inter-course with them, and quietly gave me the names of the speakers next day. And I must say they seemed to like the speeches very well.

On arriving at the hotel door I asked the policemen to take a drink, and they told me the sergeant was very watchful, but they would slip in the back way, as there was a common yard for the hotel and the barrack. They each took a half glass of whiskey and the same for their 'morning' the next day. This consorting with the hated 'Peelers' had its proper effect on those who saw it. A group of young fellows standing in front of the hotel, as I watched the crowds marching in on Sunday morning, were evidently discussing me, and one of them, looking defiantly at me over his shoulder, said: 'Ah, sure we don't care if all Scotland Yard was here.' That young man was 'on to' me and was bound to let me know it.

Davitt found me in the hall of the hotel and introduced me to J. P. Quinn,[3] then a school teacher and later Thomas Brennan's succes-sor as Secretary of the Land League. The introduction was done quietly, and Davitt and I avoided being seen together during the evening. I had also only as much talk with Quinn, who was a very bright young fellow, as was barely necessary to make connection next day.

There was a committee meeting going on in a room at the inner end of the hall and, as the talk was sometimes loud, I could hear the drift of some of it, and got occasional bulletins from young Quinn, which enabled me to keep track. Davitt was inside, and I frequently heard his voice. They were discussing the resolutions for next day's meeting, and the discussion showed the progress that had already been made.

Poor old Archbishop MacHale, then in his dotage, was being used by a group around him in an effort to stem the torrent. Canon Ulick Burke,[4] the Gaelic scholar, was in the room and had letters and telegrams from Father Tom MacHale, the Archbishop's nephew and secretary, insisting that the resolutions must include one for Catholic education and another in favour of the temporal power of the Pope, such as had been passed at public meetings in Ireland for the previous twenty years. He was told that this was to be a land meeting, that they wanted to enlist Protestants, as well as Catholics in it, and, therefore, there must be nothing sectarian in the resolutions. Canon Burke pleaded and argued, but it was all in vain. At last he said that unless they agreed to these two resolutions he could not preside at the meeting.

'Well, we're very sorry, father,' they said in substance to him, 'but the meeting must go on, and if we can't have you for chairman we must get somebody else.'

Wearied out and seeing that the men were immovable on that point, Canon Burke at last yielded and agreed to preside. There was a touch of sadness in his voice next day as he opened the meeting. I was standing in the midst of the crowd, only a few yards from the platform, with one of my 'Peeler' friends beside me and I heard every word of it.

'At Irishtown and Miltown,' said Canon Burke, 'unfortunately, priests and people were divided. Today, thank God, we stand on the same platform.'

''Deed an' we needn't thank you for that,' promptly interjected an old man standing in front of me, and just as quietly 'Thrue for you,' came from a group of seven or eight young men who evidently looked on the old man as their leader. He was a tall, stalwart man, dressed in the old-fashioned swallow-tail frieze coat, knee-breeches and leggings, and he leant on a 'cipeen' with a critical expression on his face, which, in spite of his fine physique, looked rather pinched. The young men wore more modern clothes, but they all had the same pinched look and all carried sticks.

The interruption was not made in a load voice, but it was very distinct. If Canon Burke did not catch the exact words he certainly knew it was an unfriendly remark, for he looked towards the group from which it came and it had a chilling effect. There was no animation in his speech after that. I heard later that some of his relatives were accused of being land grabbers, and that the group of men led by the old man had a special grievance against them. This surprised me very much, as I thought his work for the language would make him very popular in an Irish-speaking county. I had gone through his 'Easy Lesson in Irish', which had appeared serially in the *Nation*, but I had yet to learn that the enthusiasm for the old tongue was not in the Irish-speaking districts, but outside of them, and mainly in the cities. Although there must have been many thousands of native speakers at that meeting and many who did not understand English, I did not hear a word of Irish spoken, and there certainly was no speech, or part of speech, made in Gaelic while I was listening.

The scene as the various contingents marched into Claremorris was very exhilarating. I had seen big processions in Dublin, but never a 'monster meeting' in the country, and this one was a sight never to be forgotten. Nearly every contingent had a detachment of horsemen and all of them were marshalled by mounted men. The horses were greatly disturbed by the bands, and it was sometimes hard to keep them in line. It was very amazing to see the set faces of the mounted men as their horses reared and pranced when the banging of the drums startled them. It seemed as if the fate of Ireland depended on that old nag being kept in line, and all were certainly kept in it, but the contest between man and horse gave great amusement to the spectators.

One of the first surprises I got was seeing riding at the head of a contingent a young man living in London, whom I had met there, and who had told me that the 'New Departure' would demoralise the country. It had certainly demoralised him for that day, for he could not resist the temptation of taking part in the semi-military display. He was home on his vacation and joined the men of his native parish when they marched in. Returning to London he resumed his old attitude of antagonism to all constitutional agitation.

Every man in the procession that streamed into town wore something green. Some had green ribbons, but most of them used sprigs, and they decorated themselves in various ways. One style I had never seen before was to stretch the sprig, or the ribbon from the band at the back of the hat over the top to the band at the front. And the variety of bridle used by the cavalry was just as remarkable, many of them having only a piece of rope. But the physique was splendid, and there was fine material there for a whole division of an army. The readiness with which the men fell into line and obeyed orders gave evidence of organisation and discipline and the natural aptitude of the race for military work. The women, especially the girls, were as enthusiastic as the men, they were present in great numbers and many of them must have walked a long distance to the meeting.

That was John Dillon's[5] first attendance at a land meeting and his first speech, of which I was able to hear only a part, as I was called away. His adhesion to the movement meant a good deal for it, especially in Mayo. Although I stood near him previous to the meeting I was not introduced to him, and only met him on his arrival in America. I also saw Mr Louden[6] of Westport and James Daly of Castlebar[7] at that meeting and heard Mr Daly's speech, in which he referred to the criticisms of Archbishop MacHale about 'strolling politicians' and to Lord Oranmore and Brown,[8] who had also attacked the new movement. I also met John Walsh,[9] later an organiser, whose sister was then engaged to be married to Davitt,[10] but I had already met him with Davitt in Dublin. The most picturesque figure at the meeting was 'Scrab' Nally[11] dressed in a suit of light brown tweed, who sat on the platform and gave the signal to the boys for the applause. 'Scrab' was evidently a universal favourite and his signals were promptly obeyed. His brother, P. W. Nally, I met later in the day at another meeting.

While John Dillon was talking a hand was laid on my arm and a voice whispered in my ear: 'It's awful dry listening to these speeches. Come and get a bite to eat and something to wash it down.' I recognised the speaker, and I slipped out of the crowd with him and went to a public house, where, in an upper room, fully sixty men were gathered. They represented 3,000 organised Fenians, and were there to transact purely organisation business. They had slipped away one by one from the crowd and were not noticed. The attention of the police was directed wholly on the public meeting and, as there was absolutely no disorder, they were only interested listeners.

Although the business transacted was purely Fenian and not a word was said about the public demonstrations, that Mayo County meeting had an important bearing on the land movement and led to other action which accentuated the opposition to it among the Fenian leaders. First in order of importance was the result of the election, by which a supporter of O'Connor Power was replaced by an opponent. This change was brought about by an unwarrantable attack on the man representing Connacht on the Council of the organisation, who was not present, and which was an imputation on his character.

Some rifles had been ordered and paid for and had not been received. The fault of the delay lay with an agent in England, who was afterwards sent to penal servitude. The man who made the complaint knew that it was this man, not the Provincial Representative, who received the money and attended to the order, but his statement was worded so that the meeting understood the complaint to refer directly to the Representative. Davitt knew all the details of the matter, and as he was standing beside me, I asked him to set the meeting right. He said to me it was the Representative's duty to see that the subordinate's business was properly done, but I pointed out that this agent was under the Secretary's orders and did not even know the Representative. Davitt then promised to set them right, but somebody came up to tell him something and in the meantime the Representative was being attacked. Then I stepped forward and made the necessary explanation and there was an immediate revulsion of feeling.

The man attacked in his absence was a Mayo man, but he was then and has remained ever since a strong opponent of constitutional agitation. Davitt and he had hot arguments in Paris, and whenever they met, although they remained personally friendly, the same difference of opinion never failed to crop up. I do not claim that it was this feeling which actuated Davitt but he ought to have defended him when unjustly attacked behind his back.

The man to be selected to represent Mayo was to attend a Provincial Convention that evening and that body would choose a Representative for Connacht who would hold office for two years. I could not help thinking that this had something to do with the attack on the man whose term expired that day. But if that was the plan it failed entirely. Patrick W. Nally was elected County Centre for Mayo, and, although he had ridden at the head of a contingent to the public meeting that day and had attended the previous land meetings, he was a Fenian first and would stand by the organisation in all emergencies. His father was a man of means: he could ride his own horse or drive on his own jaunting car to any part of the county where the railroad did not connect; he was a graduate of the Galway Queen's College and was the leader of the athletes – all of which made him eminently fit for the position.

Davitt, Nally and I, with some local men, drove to Ballyhaunis on an outside car that evening, and the Provincial meeting was held there. P. J. Sheridan,[12] whom I had previously met in Dublin, represented Sligo, but the others were men who, as far as I know, have never left Ireland, so I will not name them. The Provincial Representative who had been attacked in Claremorris was re-elected.

I have often thought since that Nally's election as County Centre of Mayo, which was followed later by his election as Representative of Connacht, was the cause which led up to his arrest and conviction on perjured testimony on a charge of which he was entirely innocent, and his subsequent death in prison. I have been assured by a near relative of his, however, that I am entirely mistaken; that Pat Nally was marked for conviction anyhow, and that the perjured testimony would have been forthcoming, no matter what the charge.

When I reported the result of the County meeting at Claremorris and the Provincial one at Ballyhaunis on my return to Dublin there was great satisfaction, both among those Fenian leaders who refused to take part in the Land movement and those who were willing to help it. From the Fenian point of view it was most desirable to defeat O'Connor Power at the next Parliamentary election, and put a stop, once and for all, to Fenians going into the British Parliament, and they regarded the selection of an anti-Power man for Mayo as an unfailing indication of the result of the electoral battle. They were badly mistaken. O'Connor Power was re-elected, and this led to a renewal of the bitter feeling between Davitt and the other Fenian leaders, and gradually widened the breach.

As I left Ireland a few days after the Claremorris meeting and the events I refer to took place several months later, I cannot speak of them of my own knowledge but I heard both sides of the story fully when the two principals were in New York. When the general election came on the Fenian leaders determined that they would fight Power's election with all their energy, and it was arranged that the Secretary should go to Mayo and take private charge of the campaign. He did not go to Mayo, and this is the story he told me:

As he was about to start for the West Davitt came to him, and my recollection is that he was accompanied by Thomas Brennan, but anyhow Davitt and Brennan were going to stump Mayo. Parnell and O'Connor Power were the candidates, and according to the Secretary's statement, Davitt proposed to compromise the matter by an agreement that if the organisation would keep its hands off, he and Brennan would not say a word for Power in their speeches, but would let him take his chances with the people and do his own talking. The Secretary agreed and did not go to Mayo or have any orders issued to the men. He admitted that Davitt and Brennan kept the bargain, so far as their public speeches were concerned, but claimed that they carried on a most vigorous private canvass for Power, telling men to 'plump' for him. Further, he claimed that somebody spread the false statement that the organisation wanted O'Connor Power elected. Whether he was misinformed on this matter or not, it is an undoubted fact that there were many 'plumpers' for Power, and that he received about 100 more votes than Parnell, who was also elected. To American readers I may explain that 'plumping' meant voting the one candidate only, instead of two, every county having then two members elected at the same time.

Davitt admitted to me, in New York, that he had made the bargain with the Secretary, but indignantly denied the charge that he had broken faith. He accounted for the 'plumping' by Power's popularity in his native county and to the skilful campaign he had carried on. But he could never convince his Fenian colleagues of this, and it was the beginning of the end of their final breach with him. They consoled themselves later when Parnell found that O'Connor Power was not a loyal follower, and he was dropped from the Party, so the trouble arose over a man who was of no real use to the Land League.

I attended one more private meeting in Dublin and returned to the United States before the end of July.

Notes

Introduction

1 James Stephens, quoted in Desmond Ryan, 'Stephens, Devoy, Tom Clarke', in Conor Cruise O'Brien (ed.), *The Shaping of Modern Ireland* (London: Routledge & Kegan Paul, 1960), p. 30.

2 Thomas N. Brown, *Irish-American Nationalism, 1870–90* (Philadelphia and New York: Lippincott, 1966), p. XIV.

3 T. W. Moody, 'The New Departure in Irish politics, 1878–9', in H. A. Cronne, T. W. Moody and D. B. Quinn (eds), *Essays in British and Irish History in Honour of James Eadie Todd* (London: Muller, 1949), p. 310.

4 Michael Davitt, *The Fall of Feudalism in Ireland or the Story of the Land League Revolution* (London and New York: Harper, 1904), p. 117.

5 John Devoy, *Freeman's Journal*, 27 Dec. 1878; quoted in Ryan, 'Stephens, Devoy, Tom Clarke', p. 34.

6 Davitt evidence, *Proceedings of the Special Commission on Parnellism and Crime* (London: HMSO, 1890), vol. IX, p. 356, para. 86,565.

7 R. V. Comerford, *The Fenians in Context: Irish Politics and Society, 1848–82* (Dublin: Wolfhound, 1985), p. 225.

8 James J. O'Kelly to John Devoy, 5 August 1877, in which O'Kelly suggests Parnell as the initiator of the idea of creating a political link between parliamentarians and Fenians. See William O'Brien and Desmond Ryan (eds), *Devoy's Post Bag, 1871–1928* (Dublin: C. J. Fallon, 1948), vol. I, pp. 266–8.

9 Carroll to Patrick Mahon, 30 March 1878; quoted above, vol. I, pp. 324–5.

10 T. W. Moody, *Davitt and Irish Revolution, 1846–82* (Oxford: Oxford University Press, 1981), p. 205.

11 Davitt, *Fall of Feudalism*, pp. 111–12.

12 Moody, *Davitt*, pp. 226–49.

13 Comerford, *Fenians in Context*, p. 226.

14 See p. 43.

15 Davitt, *Fall of Feudalism*, p. 126.

16 Moody, 'The New Departure'. This remains the most thorough account of the policy.

17 F. S. L. Lyons, *Charles Stewart Parnell* (Dublin: Gill & Macmillan, 1977), p. 81.

18 Davitt, *Fall of Feudalism*, p. 136.

19 Moody, *Davitt*, p. 288.

20 M. J. Kelly, *The Fenian Ideal and Irish Nationalism, 1882–1916* (Suffolk: Boydell, 2006), p. 3.

21 Lyons, *Parnell*, pp. 81–2.

22 Parnell Evidence, *Proceedings of the Special Commission on Parnellism and Crime*, vol. VII, p. 127, para. 59,841.

23 Comerford, *Fenians in Context*, p. 224.

24 Ibid., p. 227.

25 Davitt letters to the *Freeman's Journal*, 16 Jan. 1879, 'Mr Devoy and the Freeman' and 28 Jan. 1879.

26 See for example his letter to the *Freeman's Journal*, 18 June 1880, reprinted in pamphlet form, copy in TCD MS 9360/634.

27 Davitt to Devoy, 16 Dec. 1880, reproduced in O'Brien and Ryan (eds), *Devoy's Post Bag*, vol. II, pp. 21–5.

28 Memoir of Michael Davitt by J. P. Dunne in Davitt papers, TCD MS 9465/4034 ff. 1–23.

29 John Devoy, *Land of Eire, The Irish Land League, its Origin, Progress and Consequences, preceded by a Concise History of the Various Movements Which Have Culminated in the Last Great Agitation by John Devoy, with a Descriptive and Historical Account of Ireland from the Earliest Period to the Present Day* (New York: Patterson & Neilson, 1882), pp. 90–1.

30 John Devoy, *Gaelic American*, 15 Sept. 1923; John Devoy to Patrick Ford, 10 April 1881, in O'Brien and Ryan (eds), *Devoy's Post Bag*, vol. II, pp. 62–7.

31 TCD MS 9535/40 Diary, 14 July 1882.

32 For an example of the tone of the exchanges, see *United Ireland*, 28 June 1884.

33 T. W. Moody, 'Irish American nationalism', *Irish Historical Studies*, vol. XV, no. 60 (Sept. 1967), pp. 438–45.

34 John Devoy, 'Pseudo Revolutionists trapped Davitt at the 1886 Convention', *Gaelic American*, 22 Sept. 1923, pp. 1, 5.

35 TCD MS 9545, Diary, 13 Aug. 1886.

36 See the account of the encounter by William O'Brien, one of Parnell's official delegates to the convention, in *Evening Memories* (Dublin & London: Maunsel, 1920), pp. 142–8.

37 John Devoy, *Land of Eire*. (New York: Patterson & Neilson, n.d. 1882).

38 See Terence Dooley, *The Greatest of the Fenians: John Devoy and Ireland* (Dublin: Wolfhound Press, 2003), pp. 5–6.

39 John Devoy, *Recollections of an Irish Rebel. The Fenian Movement, its Origin and Progress. Methods of Work in Ireland and in the British Army. Why it Failed to Achieve its Main Object; but Exercised Great Influence on Ireland's Future. Personalities of the Organisation. The Clan na Gael and the Rising of Easter Week, 1916. A Personal Narrative* (New York: Chas. B. Young, 1929). The New Departure is mentioned in passing twice, on pp. 313 and 344.

40 See p. 46.

41 Charles Callan Tansill, *America and the Fight For Irish Freedom, 1866–1922* (New York: Devin Adair, 1957), pp. 120–1.

42 Owen McGee, *The IRB: The Irish Republican Brotherhood from the Land League to Sinn Fein* (Dublin: Four Courts Press, 2005), pp. 298, 306, 337.

43 See above, pp. 306–7.

Obituary

1 This was the Elpis home, 19–21 Upper Mount Street, run by Margaret Huxley, where John Millington Synge was to die three years later.

2 John Dillon (1851–1927) was a friend and colleague of Davitt's since the Land League campaign. He was leader of the Anti-Parnellite wing of the Irish Parliamentary Party, 1896–1900. He had qualified as a doctor in his youth, although he did not practise.

3 Michael Davitt, Junior (1890–1928).

4 This is a mistake. Davitt was survived by four children: three sons, Michael, Cahir and Robert Emmet, and one daughter, Eileen. His eldest daughter, Kathleen, died in 1895.

5 Mary Davitt, *née* Yore (1861–1934), was born in the USA of Irish emigrant parents.

6 This is a confusion of Land League Cottage, Ballybrack, which was presented to Mary Davitt in 1887, but which the Davitts left in 1895 and St Justin's, Dalkey, Davitt's last home, which was rented.

7 The choice of St Teresa's Carmelite Church in Clarendon Street was deliberate. When in January 1878 Davitt returned to Dublin shortly after his release from prison, he was accompanied by three other former prisoners; Thomas Chambers, John Patrick O'Brien and Charles Heapy McCarthy. McCarthy died the day after his arrival and Davitt organised the funeral. McCarthy had been a Fenian and this was the only church willing to receive his body.

8   Terence Bellew McManus (1823–60), a Young Irelander, who had lived in exile in the United States. On his death in 1860, his body was brought back to Ireland for burial, the funeral providing the first large Fenian demonstration in Ireland.

9   Cardinal Paul Cullen (1803–78), Archbishop of Dublin 1852–66; he opposed Fenianism and all political movements not linked to Catholicism.

10   John O'Mahony (1816–77), a Young Irelander, founder of the Fenian organisation in the USA in 1858.

11   Cardinal Edward MacCabe (1816–85), Archbishop of Dublin, 1879–85; Cardinal, 1882. He continued his predecessor, Cardinal Cullen's policy of opposition to Fenianism and was hostile to the agrarian agitation initiated by the Land League.

12   John Redmond (1856–1918), Home Rule MP, leader of the Parnellite wing of the Irish Parliamentary Party 1891–1900; leader of the reunited party 1900–18.

13   Straide Friary was founded under the patronage of Jordan de Exeter for the Franciscan order around 1240.

14   Davitt's four surviving children were: Michael Martin (1890–1928), Eileen (1892–1974), Cahir (1894–1986) and Robert Emmet (1899–1981).

Chapter 1 Michael Davitt's career

1   C. S. Parnell's great-grandfather, Sir John Parnell, commanded a corps of the Volunteers and later strongly opposed the Act of Union.

2   This appears to be wishful thinking on Devoy's part. Davitt was certainly deeply disillusioned by the Irish Parliamentary Party and he maintained links with some Fenians throughout his life, but he showed no signs of returning to their ranks before his death.

3   The post office and printing business were owned by Henry Cockcroft.

4   There is a slight confusion here. After losing his harm, Davitt was sent, owing to the benevolence of a local cotton manufacturer, John Dean, to the local Wesleyan school in Chapel Street, Haslingden. It was on leaving this school in 1861 that he took up employment with Henry Cockcroft. However he continued his studies at night at evening classes at the Mechanics' Institute in Haslingden.

5   On 11 February 1867 the IRB launched an attack on Chester Castle in an attempt to seize arms stored there and bring them back to Ireland for use in a planned rising. The plan failed, owing to the police having been informed of it in advance.

6   In 1865 John O'Mahony, one of the founders of the Fenians, was deposed as President of the movement but he organised his own faction and the organisation split.

7   An invasion of Canada from Buffalo, New York and St Albans, Vermont, was attempted in 1866 but was driven back by the Canadians.

8   The Fenian rising took place on 5–6 March but was very limited in scale and easily defeated.

9   John Joseph Corydon, *alias* Carr (b. *c.* 1838), Fenian informer; he was later to give evidence against Davitt at Marylebone Police Court on 27 May 1870 and during his trial for treason–felony at the Old Bailey in July 1870.

10   Captain John McCafferty (1838–?), sometimes spelled McAfferty, was born in Ohio of Irish parents. He was arrested in 1865 in Dungarvan as he landed to bring arms and men for a rising in Ireland, but liberated (as an American citizen) on condition he left the country. He travelled to England late in 1866 and organised the raid on Chester Castle, but was arrested shortly afterwards and sentenced to penal servitude for life. He was released and sent to America in 1871. He may have been involved in planning the Phoenix Park murders. See William O'Brien and Desmond Ryan (eds), *Devoy's Post Bag 1871–1928* (Dublin: C. J. Fallon, 1948), vol. I, p. 37; also Michael Davitt, *The Fall of Feudalism in Ireland or the Story of the Land League Revolution* (London and New York: Harper, 1904), p. 613 and F. H. O'Donnell, *History of the Irish Parliamentary Party*, vol. II (London: Longmans, Green, 1910), pp. 273–7.

11   James Stephens (1824–1901), leader of the IRB until 1867. See Desmond Ryan, *The Fenian Chief: A Biography of James Stephens* (Dublin: Gill, 1967) and Marta Ramon, *A Provisional Dictator: James Stephens and the Fenian Movement* (Dublin: UCD Press, 2007).

12   James J. O'Kelly (1845–1916), a Dublin-born Fenian who once served on the Supreme Council, and was later a leading member of the Irish Parliamentary Party. See O'Brien and Ryan, *Devoy's Post Bag*, pp. 59–60; Devoy, *Recollections of an Irish Rebel. The Fenian Movement, its Origin and Progress. Methods of Work in Ireland and in the British Army. Why it Failed to Achieve its Main Object; but Exercised Great Influence on Ireland's Future. Personalities of the Organisation. The Clan na Gael and the Rising of Easter Week, 1916. A Personal Narrative* (New York: Chas. B. Young, 1929), pp. 333–46.

13   The Special Commission on Parnellism and Crime was set up in August 1888 in response to allegations published in *The Times* that Parnell and the Irish Parliamentary Party were involved in criminal activities.

14   He is probably referring here to the *Irish People*, founded by O'Brien in 1898, rather than *United Ireland*, of which he had earlier been editor.

15 *The Nation* – initially the organ of Young Ireland, after which Charles Gavan Duffy, its founder, sold it to A. M. Sullivan in 1855.

16 A. M. Sullivan (Alexander Martin Sullivan 1830–84): politician, barrister, poet and journalist, and editor of *The Nation*.

17 James Clancy: a London Fenian.

18 Joseph I. C. Clarke (1846–1925): Irish-American poet. His most famous poem was 'The Fighting Race' (1898).

19 John Wilson (d. 1905): the Birmingham gunsmith who was arrested with Michael Davitt on 14 May 1870.

20 Dr William Carroll (1836–1926) was the Donegal-born Chairman of the Clan na Gael executive, and one of the principal physicians in Philadelphia.

21 He left Ireland on 26 July 1878, arriving on 4 August.

22 *The Herald* (New York) was owned by Gordon Bennett. Devoy was its foreign editor.

23 See William O'Brien and Desmond Ryan (eds), *Devoy's Post Bag, 1871–1928*, vol. I, pp. 354–68 for letters relating to this lecture tour.

24 Patrick Ford (1837–1913): journalist and politician, was the Irish-born editor of the *Irish World*, an influential weekly Irish-American paper.

Chapter 2 Davitt's relations with the Fenians 1

1 John B. Mitchel (1815–75) was a member of Young Ireland, transported to Tasmania in 1848, from which he escaped in 1853, thereafter living in the United States. He was revered in radical national circles and is best known for his *Jail Journal* (1854).

2 James Fintan Lalor (1807–49) was an advocate of nationalist principles in the 1840s. He contributed articles to the *Nation* (1847) on land and is chiefly known for his radical views on the land question.

3 Davitt spent April to June 1897 in the USA, lobbying senators against a proposed Anglo-American Arbitration Treaty, which was defeated.

4 *The Spectator* is a British conservative weekly; sister paper of the *Daily Telegraph*. It has been published continuously since 1828.

5 Davitt's diaries were never published but are among the Davitt papers in the Manuscripts Library, Trinity College Dublin.

6 Davitt's mother, Catherine, *née* Kielty, had moved to Manayunk; a small industrial suburb of Pennsylvania, from Scranton in 1873.

7 This took place on Sunday, 18 August 1878.

8 This was on 23 September 1878.

9   John J. Breslin (1836–88) was a hospital steward in Richmond Prison who helped James Stephens escape on 24 November 1865. He emigrated to the United States and played a leading part in Clan na Gael. He was Business Manager of Devoy's paper, the *Irish Nation*, in the 1880s.

10   This was held on 13 October 1878, so in fact it took place three weeks later. Devoy's memory, over a quarter of a century after the event, is a little inaccurate about the interval between meetings.

11   William Sharman Crawford (1781–1861) was a Protestant landlord in Co. Down and MP, best known for his advocacy of legislation on tenant right. He formed the Ulster Tenant Association in 1846 and the Tenant League in 1850.

12   Isaac Butt (1813–79) was an economist and barrister, founder and editor of the *Dublin University Magazine*, and MP. He founded the Home Rule Association in 1870 and was chairman of the Home Rule Party 1874–9. He was also Head of the Amnesty Association and of the Tenant League. The 'Three Fs': fixity of tenure, fair rent and free sale of tenant right were the standard demands of the tenant right movement in the 1860s and 1870s.

13   William Erigena Robinson (1814–92) of Brooklyn, New York. Born Co. Tyrone, he served as Democratic Party representative for New York in 1867–9 and 1881–5.

14   This was, in fact, only four days after the Brooklyn meeting.

15   The *Boston Pilot* was a nationalist weekly paper owned and edited by John Boyle O'Reilly (1844–90): a Fenian transported to Western Australia in 1868; escaped in 1869 in the *Catalpa* rescue. Arriving in Boston he found work on the *Pilot*, of which he became editor and proprietor in 1870. He was well known as a poet and author of the novel, *Moondyne* (1879).

Chapter 3 Davitt and the Fenians

1   Thomas Power O'Connor MP (1848–1929): journalist and newspaper editor, politician and author.

2   Mary Canning (*née* Morgan) was Mary Davitt's aunt, who raised her in Oakland, California, after the death of her mother. She died in 1904, leaving her niece a legacy sufficient to enable the Davitts to live in comfort.

3   Thomas Nicholas Burke (1830–83): Dominican friar. He became immensely popular as a preacher and lecturer and raised £100,000 for American charities. His most famous lectures were delivered on the relations between Ireland and England.

4   *Irish American*: weekly newspaper published in New York, 1849–1915.

5   John Boyle O'Reilly, see ibid., chapter 2 note 15.

6 General P. A. Collins (1844–1905), born in Fermoy, Co. Cork, became a Boston-based Irish-American; a conservative member of Clan na Gael and friend of John Boyle O'Reilly. He served as second President of the American Land League, thereafter a member of Congress, Consul General in London and Mayor of Boston (1901–5).

7 Dr Robert Dwyer Joyce (1830–83): born Limerick, was a poet and physician and a friend of O'Reilly.

8 Archbishop John Joseph Williams of Boston (1822–1907): first Catholic Archbishop of Boston; originally co-owner, with O'Reilly, of the Boston *Pilot*.

9 See Davitt's letter to Devoy, in NLI MS 18003, dated 'Friday evening', 1878; reproduced in William O'Brien and Desmond Ryan (eds), *Devoy's Post Bag, 1871–1928* (Dublin: C. J. Fallon, 1948), vol. I, p. 356.

10 This was Thomas J. Mooney. Devoy in a further reference to Mooney in *Gaelic American*, 25 June 1923, refers to him as having left Ireland under a cloud because of 'some financial difficulty in 1848'. John T. McEnnis in *Clan na Gael and the Murder of Dr Cronin* (Chicago: F. J. Schulte & J. W. Iliff, 1889) claims that 'Mooney' was an alias for James Moorehead, who took part in the dynamite campaign in London and Glasgow in March and April 1883, or claimed to, although Davitt attributed this to others (Michael Davitt, *The Fall of Feudalism in Ireland or the Story of the Land League Revolution* (London and New York: Harper, 1904), pp. 428–34). See O'Brien and Ryan (eds), *Devoy's Post Bag*, vol. I, p. 194.

11 See W. L. Feingold, *The Revolt of the Tenantry: The Transformation of Local Government in Ireland, 1875–86* (Boston: Northeastern University Press, 1984)

12 Thomas B. Connery was Managing Director of the *New York Herald* and a personal friend of Devoy.

13 Jerome J. Collins (1841–81): journalist and pioneering meteorologist. He died tragically on an expedition to Siberia in October 1881.

14 Established in 1841 by Horace Greely, The *Tribune* had been a radical Republican newspaper during the Civil War but was taken over in 1872 by Whitelaw Reid, who owned the *New York Herald*. In 1924 the two papers were merged to form the *New York Herald Tribune*.

15 The *New York Times* was founded in 1851 as a daily paper by Henry Jarvis Raymond.

16 The *New York World* was published from 1860 to 1931. It was innovative in style and competed for readers with Randolph Hearst's *New York American*. The *New York Sun* commenced publication as a daily paper in 1833 and continued until 1919, when it was subsumed into the *New York Herald*. Davitt contributed letters to it in the 1880s and 1890s.

17 'Meleady' in the original. See NLI MS 18003, Davitt to Devoy. Patrick Meledy was one of the eight Fenian prisoners who remained in custody after Davitt's release. He and two others travelled to the USA on their release, arriving in New York on 28 September, where Davitt was present at their reception. See T. W. Moody, *Davitt and Irish Revolution, 1846–82* (Oxford: Oxford University Press, 1981), p. 235.

18 Patrick Mahon of Rochester, N.Y., Treasurer of Clan na Gael until his death in 1881.

Chapter 4 Davitt's relations with the Fenians 11

1 Logan in the original letter. See NLI MS 18003, Davitt to Devoy, 'Friday evening' [1 October 1878]; reproduced in William O'Brien and Desmond Ryan (eds), *Devoy's Post Bag, 1871–1928* (Dublin: C. J. Fallon, 1948), vol. I, pp. 355–6.

2 Hogan in the original letter. Probably Martin J. Hogan.

3 McGuinness in the original letter.

4 Joseph Gillis Biggar (1828–90): Home Rule MP, member of IRB 1875–7, and originator of policy of obstruction in House of Commons.

5 General F. F. Millen was Chairman of the Fenian Military Council in 1865. He acted as deputy to Stephens when he was imprisoned. He emigrated to New York in 1871 and became a member of the Clan na Gael Executive Committee. According to Owen McGee, *The IRB: The Irish Republican Brotherhood from the Land League to Sinn Fein* (Dublin: Four Courts Press, 2005), pp. 105, 133, he was a spy for the British Special Branch.

6 Thomas Clarke Luby (1821–68) was a member of Young Ireland and later a founder of the IRB. After serving a term of imprisonment from 1865–71, he settled in New York, where he joined Clan na Gael.

7 General Thomas Francis Bourke (1840–89) was born in Wexford but settled in New York where he joined the Fenian Brotherhood. He travelled to Ireland to take part in the Fenian Rising. His sentence to death was commuted to imprisonment for life but he was released in 1871 and returned to the USA, where he was active in Clan na Gael and the Land League.

8 Charles Joseph Kickham (1828–82): Young Irelander and Fenian. Served as President of the Supreme Council of the IRB *c.*1873–82. Famous as a novelist and author of *Knocknagow* (Dublin: James Duffy, 1879).

9 George Henry Moore MP (1811–70), was a supporter of tenant right, founder of the Catholic Defence Association and leader of the Irish Brigade. He participated in the formation of the Independent Irish Party.

10 John 'Amnesty' Nolan (d. 1887) was a Fenian; Secretary of the Amnesty Association. Nolan left Dublin for New York in 1875 and died there. Davitt erected a monument to his memory in Glasnevin.

11 'Manchester Rescue': on 18 September 1867 Fenians were rescued from a prison van in Manchester, during which incident the guard, Sergeant Brett, was shot dead.

12 'Whig' was a term used disparagingly by Fenians to describe moderate Home Rulers.

Chapter 5 Michael Davitt and the Clan na Gael

1 Jeremiah O'Donovan Rossa (1831–1915) was a nationalist and early member of the IRB. Arrested in 1865 he was sentenced to 20 years' penal servitude but released in 1871, after enduring harsh treatment. He emigrated to the USA, where he edited the *United Irishman* and participated in planning the dynamite campaign in Britain. In November 1869, he ran successfully as a candidate in a by-election in Tipperary as a protest against his imprisonment, but was deemed ineligible to take his seat, as an unpardoned felon.

2 See above, chapter 2 note 1. In 1874, Mitchel was elected MP for Tipperary but was declared ineligible to take his seat as an undischarged felon. However, he was re-elected for the same constituency in 1875.

3 Frank Hugh O'Donnell (1848–1916), author and politician. Foreign editor of the *Morning Post*. MP for Galway 1874 but unseated on petition. MP for Dungarvan 1877–85 but Parnell refused to allow him be nominated in 1885, whereupon he retired from politics. He was antagonistic to Parnell.

4 See above, chapter 2 note 9; Breslin had led the Catalpa mission to rescue six Fenian prisoners from Australia in 1876.

5 See above, chapter 4 note 7.

Chapter 6 Returned to Ireland to open campaign

1 This meeting seems to have been held in Boston, and not in New York, as Devoy asserts here. See T. W. Moody, *Davitt and Irish Revolution, 1846–82* (Oxford: Oxford University Press, 1981), p. 259.

2 See above, chapter 3 note 7; Joyce's novel, *Deirdre*, was published in 1876.

3 On 5 March 1867, during the Fenian rising, a section of Dublin Fenians made its way to Tallaght, where they were intercepted by a party of constabulary and after an exchange of fire the Fenians were dispersed. See Kevin B. Nowlan, 'The Fenian Rising', in T. W. Moody (ed.), *The Fenian Movement* (Cork & Dublin: Mercier, 1968), pp. 23–35.

4   This was a reference to the abortive rising in 1848, led by William Smith O'Brien, which was pejoratively referred to as 'the affray in the Widow McCormack's cabbage patch'.

5   This referred to the demand for a simple repeal of the Act of Union, which had been the programme of Daniel O'Connell in the 1840s.

6   John O'Connor (1850–1928), was secretary of the IRB Supreme Council and a grocer-publican from Cork. He was elected MP for Tipperary County in 1885.

7   J. C. Flynn was MP for Cork North from 1885 to 1910.

8   Patrick Joseph Sheridan was a hotel keeper in Tubbercurry and Fenian County Centre for Sligo. Although an early opponent of the New Departure, he became one of the leading organisers of the land agitation in the West.

9   *Saunders' News Letter and Irish Daily News* was published from 1828 to 1878, when it was continued as *Saunders' Irish Daily News*, until its final issue on 24 November 1879.

Chapter 7 Davitt meets the Fenian leaders in Paris

1   Thomas Brennan (1854–1915) was probably Davitt's closest friend; a member of the IRB, later full-time secretary to the Land League. He was opposed to the Kilmainham Treaty and emigrated in 1882 to Nebraska, where he prospered as an estate agent.

2   Built in 1855 and originally located in the building which is now known as the Louvre des Antiquaires, the Hotel du Louvre was the first luxury hotel in France. It is situated in what is today called the Place Andre Malraux, opposite the Louvre. It was a grand hotel with 700 guestrooms and a large staff of 1,250. The Hotel du Louvre was then relocated to the other side of the square where it stands today, enjoying its prime position with each of the four façades offering a different outlook.

3   The hotel was named after a seventeenth-century seminary on the Rue du Bac.

4   He is probably referring to John O'Connor.

5   John O'Connor Power (1846–1919), was a Fenian, expelled from the IRB Supreme Council after his election as MP for Mayo County in 1874.

6   Moody names them as the eleven members of the Supreme Council and Devoy, who was specially admitted as the representative of Clan na Gael. The names of eight of the eleven members are known: Kickham (President), John O'Connor (Secretary), O'Leary, Davitt, Matthew Harris, John Ryan, Mark Ryan and John Torley. Of the three unnamed members, he suggests that two may possibly have been Robert Johnson and P. N. Fitzgerald. Moody, *Davitt*, p. 278.

7 Andrew Fletcher of Saltoun (1653–1716): Scottish writer, politician and patriot, was known for his remark: 'I knew a very wise man so much of Sir Christopher's sentiment, that he believed if a man were permitted to make all the ballads, he need not care who should make the laws of a nation.'

8 In 1871, at the age of 24, O'Connor Power entered St Jarleth's College, Tuam, to acquire a secondary education. He remained there until 1874.

9 On 23 November 1867, three Fenians, Allan, Larkin and O'Brien, were hanged for the murder of a prison guard, Sergeant Brett, in the course of the rescue of other Fenians from a prison van in Manchester. Their execution became the focus for an annual nationalist commemoration.

Chapter 8 The Paris conference ended amicably

1 John Martin (1812–75) was a Young Irelander who founded the *Irish Felon* to replace Mitchel's *United Irishman*. Sentenced to transportation to Van Diemen's Land (Tasmania), he was pardoned and in 1856 returned to Ireland. He was elected Home Rule MP for Co Meath in 1871 and served as Secretary to the Home Rule League.

2 Devoy may be mistaken here because in 1871 when the election took place, Dr Bartholomew Woodlock was Rector of the Catholic University College in Dublin. He was not appointed Bishop of Ardagh and Clonmacnoise until 1879.

3 Alexander Martin Sullivan (1830–84): politician, barrister, poet and journalist; he was editor of *The Nation* (1855–77).

4 Matthew Harris (1825–90) was a remarkable political activist based in Ballinasloe Co Galway. He was successively a Chartist, a Young Irelander, a tenant right activist, a Fenian, a Land League leader and a Home Rule MP.

5 George Sigerson (1836–1925) was a physician, scientist, journalist and writer. He encouraged Irish literature and music and lived to be one of the first members of the Free State Senate.

6 James O'Connor (1836–1910) was a Fenian and a friend of Kickham. Sentenced to ten years' penal servitude as a member of the staff of the *Irish People*, he was released in 1869 and became the chief writer on the *Irishman*. The telegram from Devoy to Parnell setting out the terms of the 'New Departure' had been sent initially to O'Connor with instructions to pass it on to Kickham.

7 William Shaw (1823–95) was a minister of the Congregational Church in Cork and then entered business. He was an MP (1868–85) and was elected Chairman of the Irish Party following Butt's death in 1879, but lost the leadership to Parnell in 1880.

8 Mitchell Henry was MP for Galway County, 1871–85.

9 Sir Joseph Neale McKenna was MP for New Ross (1859–63), Youghal (1865–8, 1874–85) and Monaghan South (1885–92).

10 William O'Brien (1852–1928): journalist, writer and politician, first made his name as a journalist on the *Freeman's Journal*. Parnell appointed him editor of *United Ireland* in 1881. He was one of the leaders of the Plan of Campaign and the founder of the United Irish League.

11 Little glasses.

Chapter 9 Parnell's relations with Clan na Gael

1 This was John O'Leary (1830–1907): from a Catholic middle-class family in Tipperary. A nationalist who was opposed to the Land League and went on to support Parnell in the 1890–1 election.

2 The point of Kickham's remark here was that O'Leary was a religious sceptic whose appreciation of cathedrals was purely aesthetic.

3 Louis Léon César Faidherbe (1818–89) was a French general and colonial administrator. He served in Algeria, West Indies and Senegal, and was recalled to France in 1870 during the Franco-Prussian War, winning several small victories against the Prussian First Army at the towns of Ham, Hallue, Pont-Novelles, and Bapaume.

4 It was John O'Leary.

5 Sergeant Charles 'Heapy' McCarthy: a former soldier and Fenian, was held in Chatham prison. On his release in January 1878, he travelled with Chambers, Davitt and O'Brien to Dublin, amid large demonstrations. He died a few days after his arrival.

6 Corporal Thomas Chambers was a former soldier and Fenian, who was in Dartmoor with Davitt and was released in January 1878.

7 W. H. O'Sullivan: MP for Limerick County, 1874–85.

8 F. H. O'Donnell, see above, chapter 5 note 3.

9 John O'Connor (1850–1928), Secretary of IRB Supreme Council.

10 O'Leary.

11 Rt. Hon. Edward Gibson, QC, Lord Ashbourne (1837–1913), Conservative MP for Waterford City (1874) and for Dublin University (1875–85); Attorney General 1877–80; Lord Chancellor (1885–6, 1886–92, 1895–1905).

12 John Patrick O'Brien was a former soldier and Fenian released with Charles McCarthy from Chatham prison early in January 1878.

13 Rev. Professor Joseph A. Galbraith was a Fellow of Trinity College, an economist, and a member of the Home Rule Association. He is the man credited with inventing the term 'Home Rule'.

Chapter 10 With Parnell and Biggar in Boulogne

1   The Hotel de Seine still exists on 52 Rue de Seine. It is a large, 30-bedroom hotel and probably a good deal more luxurious than it was in Devoy's day.

2   This was around the middle of March 1879.

3   Delia Tudor Stewart Parnell (1816–98), American mother of Charles Stewart Parnell.

4   Fanny Parnell (1849–82), poet and journalist. Founder of the American Ladies' Land League.

5   Charles Stewart Vane-Tempest Stewart, Sixth Marquess of Londonderry (1852–1915). As Viscount Castlereagh, he was returned as MP for County Down in 1878 and held the seat until the death of his father in 1884, when he took a seat in the House of Lords as Earl Vane. Devoy's antipathy to the name Castlereagh arose from the fact that his ancestor, the Second Marquess of Londonderry, Lord Castlereagh, was one of the architects of the Act of Union.

6   James Sharman Crawford was the eldest son of William Sharman Crawford, the campaigner for tenant right. He was a Liberal MP for Co. Down from 1874 until his death in 1878.

Chapter 11 Sought alliances with foreign powers

1   Simon Barclay Conover: U.S. Senator (1873–79).

2   Edwin W. Stoughton from New York served as US Ambassador to Russia from 30 October 1877 to 2 March 1879.

3   Emilio Castelar y Ripoll (1832–99): politician, writer and last President of the First Spanish Republic.

4   Estanislau Figueras (1819–82) was a Catalan politician and the First President of the First Spanish Republic (11 Feb.–11 June 1873). He briefly became President after King Amadeo abdicated. He was succeeded as President by Franceso Pi y Margall. After the 1875 restoration of the monarchy he withdrew from public life.

5   Francisco Pi y Margall (1824–1901) was a liberal Spanish statesman and Catalan romanticist writer. He was briefly President of the short-lived First Spanish Republic in 1873.

6   Antonio Cánovas Del Castillo (1828–97): Spanish politician and historian, known principally for his role in supporting the restoration of the Bourbon Monarchy to the Spanish throne and for his death at the hands of an anarchist assassin – Michele Angiolillo. He served as Spanish Prime Minister for several terms between 1874 and his death in 1897.

Chapter 12 On the eve of the Land League in 1879

1   Thomas Francis Meagher (1823–67), member of the Repeal Association and founder member of the Irish Confederation. Arrested for rising in 1848, he was sent to Van Diemen's Land (Tasmania), whence he escaped to America in 1852 and became a journalist. Organised an Irish brigade on the Northern side in the American Civil War.

2   Morrison's Hotel was an elegant hotel at the bottom of Dawson Street. Parnell favoured it over the more shabby Imperial Hotel on O'Connell Street patronised by most of the Irish nationalist leadership.

Chapter 13 The agitation launched at Irishtown

1   Thomas Brennan, see above, chapter 7 note 1.

2   Moody puts the first of these on 6 April and the second on 1 June. Davitt suggests that the first meeting was at Egan's house in Synott Place but Devoy is certain they were both at Morrison's hotel, and Moody argues that his account is the more detailed and likely to be the more accurate. See T. W. Moody, *Davitt and Irish Revolution, 1846–82* (Oxford: Oxford University Press, 1981), p. 288.

3   1847: 'Black 47' the worst year of the Great Famine.

4   This was James Daly. See Gerard Moran, 'James Daly and the rise and fall of the Land League in the West of Ireland, 1879–82', *Irish Historical Studies*, vol. XXIX, no. 114 (Nov. 1994), pp. 189–207.

5   Cetshwayo, or Cetewayo (1826–84): the last great king of the Zulus, ruled 1873–9. As leader of an army of 40,000 men he was considered a threat to British colonial interests and his power was destroyed in the Zulu War which was taking place in 1879.

6   John O'Kane, a shopkeeper in Claremorris, was one of the first organisers of the Irishtown meeting.

7   Patrick W. Nally was a farmer from Balla. He was the champion athlete of Mayo and an ardent Fenian. Sentenced to ten years penal servitude in 1882, he died in Mountjoy Jail on 9 November 1891.

8   Benjamin Disraeli: 1st Earl of Beaconsfield (1804–81): Prime Minister and leader of the Conservative Party.

Chapter 14 How Parnell accepted the leadership

1   Michael Davitt, *The Fall of Feudalism in Ireland or the Story of the Land League Revolution* (London and New York: Harper, 1904), pp. 176–7, actually places the first and not the second meeting at Egan's house, but see above, chapter 12 note 2.

2   Parnell's grandfather, Commodore Charles Stewart (1778–1869), was a commander in the American navy, his most famous engagement being in the war with Britain in 1812, in which he captured two British ships off the coast of Spain, for which he became a national hero.

3   He is referring to Henry Parnell (1776–1842), who entered the Irish House of Commons in 1797 and opposed the Union. He was later elected to the British House of Commons and published a *History of the Penal Laws* (1808). He was Charles Stewart Parnell's grand uncle.

4   Lugnaquilla is the highest peak in the Wicklow mountains and the highest in Leinster.

5   This appears to be a broad hint that he was not the author of the topographical section of *Land of Eire, The Irish Land League, its Origin, Progress and Consequences, preceded by a Concise History of the Various Movements Which Have Culminated in the Last Great Agitation by John Devoy, with a Descriptive and Historical Account of Ireland from the Earliest Period to the Present Day* (New York: Patterson & Neilson, 1882)

6   P. J. Smyth (1826–85), at this time Home Rule MP for Co. Westmeath. Davitt privately referred to him as an 'Irish national Don Quixote'. See TCD MS 9639, published in edited form as Michael Davitt, *Jottings in Solitary*, ed. C. King (Dublin: UCD Press, 2003), p. 158.

7   See above, chapter 8 note 5.

8   Richard Barry O'Brien (1847–1918): author of the first major biography of Parnell, *The Life of Charles Stewart* Parnell (London: Smith, Elder, & Co. 1898).

9   In early December 1890 the Irish Parliamentary Party split in the wake of the granting of a decree nisi to Captain O'Shea, naming Parnell as co-defendant. Davitt was one of the leaders of the anti-Parnell side.

10   Three resolutions, written by Davitt, were put to the meeting at Irishtown and carried. The first made a claim to self-government for Ireland; the second condemned landlordism; and the third called for an immediate reduction of unjust rents pending a settlement of the Land Question.

11   John Sadleir (1815–56) was MP for Carlow (1847–53) and Sligo (1853–6), and a leader of the Irish Brigade at Westminster. He was also a key figure in the Catholic Defence Association (nicknamed the 'Pope's Brass Band'). His

acceptance of the post of Lord of the Treasury in December 1852 was believed to undermine the Independent Irish Party.

Chapter 15 Conditions which Parnell agreed to

1 The Special Commission on Parnellism and Crime, 1888–9.

2 Henry George (1839–97), land reformer and economist. His most influential work, *Progress and Poverty* was first published in 1879, advocated the nationalisation of land, on which a tax should be charged. Davitt and George met in New York in 1880 and in 1881–2 he was Irish correspondent for the *Irish World*. He published a pamphlet, *The Irish Land Question: What it Involves and How Alone it Can be Settled: An Appeal to the Land Leagues* (New York, 1879 and London 1881).

3 See above, chapter 2 note 2.

4 John MacHale (1791–1881): Archbishop of Tuam, a strong supporter of Catholic Emancipation and of Irish culture and language. Opposed to national school system and Queen's colleges.

5 On Saturday, 7 June a letter from the Archbishop was published in the *Freeman's Journal* warning Catholics not to attend a meeting 'convened in a mysterious and disorderly manner' and 'organised by a few designing men'.

Chapter 16 Why the Fenians were hostile to Sullivan

1 See above, chapter 8 note 3.

2 William Smith O'Brien (1803–64): nationalist, leading member of Young Ireland and founder of Irish Convention. He led an abortive rising in 1848 at Ballingarry, Co Tipperary (see above, chapter 6 note 4), for which he was sentenced to death, commuted to penal servitude for life. He served five years in Tasmania, returning to Ireland in 1856.

3 This refers to a process server named Daniel Sullivan Goula who was the most prominent informer in trials of Jeremiah O'Donovan Rossa and others connected with the *Phoenix*.

4 In October 1858, Fr John O'Sullivan of Kenmare: Vicar-General of Kerry diocese, discovered that a conspiracy had been imported into his parish from the Skibbereen area. He informed the local magistrate and denounced the conspiracy from the pulpit at Sunday mass.

5 See above, *Obituary* note 8.

6 Daniel O'Donoghue, styled The O'Donoghue, Chieftain of the Glens, claimed chieftainship of the O'Donoghue Clan and was a grandnephew of

Daniel O'Connell. Elected MP for Tipperary in 1858, he became a leader of the independent Irish Party at Westminster and was an extremely popular figure.

7   See above, chapter 8 note 1.

8   Ribbonmen were local agrarian secret societies which engaged in intimidation and violence.

9   Philip Callan, MP for Dundalk (1868–80); MP for Co. Louth (1880–5); for North Louth (1885, 1892); for Louth South (1896).

10   Timothy Daniel Sullivan (1827–1914): MP, politician and poet and brother of A. M. Sullivan.

Chapter 17   The great Claremorris land meeting

1   See above, chapter 4 note 5.

2   See above, chapter 7 note 1.

3   Joseph Patrick Quinn of Claremorris was at this time a schoolteacher and Fenian. He later served as Secretary of the Land League and was imprisoned with Parnell in Kilmainham in October 1881 and with Davitt and T. M. Healy in 1883. He eventually qualified as a doctor and became medical officer to the South Dublin Union.

4   Ulick J. Bourke (1829–87), priest and teacher. First Chairman of the Society for the Preservation of the Irish language.

5   See *Obituary* note 2.

6   John James Louden, B. L., of Westport; Chairman of the Mayo Tenants' Defence Association and a founder of the Mayo Land League. He became a member of the Committee of the Irish National Land League.

7   James Daly of Castlebar (1835/6–1910): editor of *Connaught Telegraph*, leader of tenant right agitation in Connaught 1876–8 and Secretary of Mayo Tenants' Defence Association. He was a founder of the Mayo Land League and served on the Committee of the Irish National Land League.

8   Geoffrey Browne, Lord Oranmore and Browne (1819–1900), 2nd Baron, alluded in the House of Lords to 'meetings of a communistic character' lately held in Ireland. See *Hansard*, 3: CXXLIV, 817: CCXLVI, 1428–9, 1898.

9   John W. Walshe of Balla: a cousin of Davitt. An early organiser of the Land League and Secretary of the Mayo Land League and became a local organiser for the Irish National Land League.

10   Beatrice Walshe – she played an important part in the Ladies' Land League but later emigrated with her brother to Australia.

11   John William ('Scrab') Nally. He was John Walshe's brother in law; a publican in Balla.

12   See above, chapter 6 note 8.